Personal Computer
Buying Guide

Personal Computer Buying Guide

Foolproof Advice on
How to Buy
Computer Software and Hardware

Olen R. Pearson

and the Editors of Consumer Reports Books

Consumers Union
Mount Vernon, New York

Library of Congress Cataloging-in-Publication Data
Pearson, Olen R.
    Personal computer buying guide : foolproof advice on how to buy
    computer software and hardware / by Olen R. Pearson and the editors
    of Consumer Reports Books.
      p. cm.
    Includes index.
    ISBN 0-89043-336-4 (pbk.)
    1. Microcomputers—Purchasing.   I. Consumer Reports Books.
    II. Title.
    QA76.5.P369   1990
    004.16′029′7—dc20   90-2002
                                     CIP
                                     Rev.

Design by GDS / Jeffrey L. Ward
First printing, September 1990
Manufactured in the United States of America

Consumer Reports Books

To my mother,
who always believes in me,
even when I don't deserve it,
which is probably much too often!

□ □ □ □ □

Contents

□ □ □ □ □

Acknowledgments

While the idea for this book was my own, it might well have never been written without the encouragement, support, and many helpful comments and suggestions from my family, friends, and colleagues. To those who unselfishly contributed their time and energy to the improvement of this book and the preservation of my sanity, I am indebted.

I also wish to express my special appreciation to the editors and staff of Consumer Reports Books for their confidence in this project as well as their most capable guidance and assistance in converting my technical jargon into a readable presentation.

—O.R.P.

The Editors of Consumer Reports Books give special thanks to A. Larry Seligson for reviewing the contents of this book.

Personal Computer
Buying Guide

□ □ □ □ □

Introduction

The first microcomputer designed for personal use was introduced little more than a decade ago. In 1975, the Altair 8800 was announced, but this was available only in a kit form and was of interest mainly to the electronics hobbyist and computer enthusiast. There soon followed models by such now familiar names as Apple, Atari, Commodore, and Tandy (Radio Shack), which were suitable for anyone, whether or not they'd had any prior experience with computers. The floodgates were then open, never again to be closed.

The early 1980s saw an explosion in the number of companies offering personal computers. Many firms withdrew from the field because of either an inferior product or the inability to market their wares successfully against intense competition. IBM was somewhat late entering the microcomputer race, not introducing its first PC until September 1981. However, its leadership in the personal computer market was soon firmly established. After IBM's successful entry into this rapidly growing market, a number of IBM clones or compatibles were introduced that now permeate the market.

The early microcomputers, although inferior to today's standards, were marvels for their time. For the first time you could bring the power of a computer into your home, office, or business without connecting into a large mainframe system—and at a reasonable cost. After only a few years, personal systems have become so powerful that many will now outperform some of the large computers of little more than a decade ago.

Consumer choice from among the earlier systems was limited. There were only a few places to buy your computer and a restricted selection of models and accessories. Today, not only do computer and most electronics stores carry microcomputers, but there are numerous other places to shop, including many department, toy, and office supply stores. There is also a truly mind-boggling array of models, options, accessories, add-ons, and so forth, from which to choose to build your computer system. This book is intended to help lead you through this potentially confusing landscape to arrive at an informed and appropriate selection for your computer system, one that suits your wants and needs as closely as possible.

Although certain computers are sometimes mentioned by name as examples, no specific brand or model will be analyzed or recommended. The microcomputer world is changing so rapidly that models discussed today may be outdated or even out of production in a short time, in favor of more powerful systems. This book discusses the basic capabilities and general features of microcomputers, as well as their major accessories, in straightforward, nontechnical terms.

This book outlines the basic steps and introduces you to the essential vocabulary that will help you select the best system for your needs. Chapter 1 outlines the seven basic steps that will take you through the process of preparing for and making your purchase. In the chapters that follow you will learn such things as how to gather information, compare and select equipment, and set up and care for your system once you get it home. Finally, a comprehensive Mini-Dictionary is included to assist you in understanding the required terminology.

In addition, three appendices are provided to assist you. The Manufacturers Resource Guide provides addresses and telephone numbers for most of the more popular computer product manufacturers. Most of these companies will provide literature or answer specific questions on their products upon request. The second appendix provides four checklists that can assist you in assessing your needs, selecting software and hardware, and evaluating dealers. The final appendix is a reprint of a *Consumer Reports* product Ratings report on the laptop, which is one of the fastest growing and evolving types of computers in today's market.

1

□ □ □ □ □

Seven Basic Steps

What is the best computer to buy? Of course, there is no single best computer, no specific manufacturer's model that best suits everyone's needs. The best computer for you is the one that best fits your individual needs. If an inexpensive system does not have the capabilities to run the software packages that you wish to use, then you will almost certainly be dissatisfied with it and may either give up in frustration or end up spending additional money for the more powerful system that you could have purchased in the first place. Such a misadventure would end up costing more than if you had purchased the more expensive system to begin with. On the other hand, buying a system that has many times the computing power and features you need or want can be just as wasteful.

It is very important to establish your needs and ascertain what equipment is available to fit those needs before you can decide what type of computer and accessories are best for you. Few people would buy a car without first having driven it, yet many people purchase a personal computer without first giving it a "test run" to see if it's comfortable for them or if it's right for their needs. This is why it's crucial to become **computer literate,** or knowledgeable, about computers and your needs.

Here are the basic steps that you should follow when planning for your system:

1. Become computer literate.
2. Learn what is available.
3. Thoroughly assess your needs.
4. Select your software.

3

5. Select your hardware.
6. Buy intelligently.
7. Use, maintain, and care for your investment.

Each step is related to and dependent on the others. For example, you can't adequately assess your needs until you become informed about computers and what is available. But how much you need to learn and in what areas depends significantly on what you intend to do with your computer—for example, whether you'll be running a word processor, spreadsheet, or educational software.

Let's look briefly at what each of these steps involves.

Step 1. Become Computer Literate

Becoming computer literate basically involves three things: (1) learning the terminology or language **(computerese)** surrounding computers, (2) learning what is available in basic equipment and accessories, and (3) gaining some hands-on experience. Do not underestimate the importance of the last item. It is not uncommon for someone to become very knowledgeable about computers yet remain so intimidated by or afraid of them **(computerphobic)** that the new system remains virtually untouched because of fear.

There are many sources available to help you learn about computers. The Mini-Dictionary at the end of this book will help you learn computerese. Your local library and bookstore can provide other books and magazines, both on general as well as more specialized topics. Also, if there are computers available at your work, school, friends' homes, or at other places where you have access, you may be able to gain some of the all-important hands-on experience.

Step 2. Learn What Is Available

As you become computer literate, you will learn much about which computers and accessories are available and what they are capable of doing, enough to know at least what you will need and where to look for further information. The wealth of sources available provides more information than you will need, so it is essential to narrow your focus.

Make a list of your "wants" or "would likes." When you find something that interests you, add it to your list. You can then look for further information on those particular items. You should be able to gain a rough idea of the cost of each item that you want and thus what the total system will cost you.

Step 3. Thoroughly Assess Your Needs

Your "want list"—which may change several times—should summarize your requirements and lead you to final judgments as to your true needs.

Rigorously edit your "want list" in light of the projected cost. For example, if the only requirement you have for color and graphics is a few games you will play only occasionally, it may be that with the cost of the extra hardware required to obtain the color graphics, the games are not a justified expense. Remember, the software and hardware must be carefully matched, a point to be discussed in detail.

The danger of buying a system far beyond your needs is equal to that of buying one so simple that it cannot even meet your present requirements. But people and their needs change. As you use your system you may discover that you want to do things you consider out of the question now. Keep in mind that you may want to add more items in the future. Factor in the capability for expansion. Perhaps you are not sure about games now but would like to leave that option open as a future possibility; be sure any system will permit you to add color and graphics later if you should decide that you want to have the games. Consider only those systems that offer adequate expansion potential.

Step 4. Select Your Software

Software should be selected first. Many people make the mistake of purchasing the hardware first, under the assumption that the software they want will be available. Unfortunately, this is not always the case, and some of these buyers become disappointed and discouraged when their system does not meet their needs.

There are two basic reasons for selecting your software first. First, it is primarily the software that determines the applications that will run on your system, and this is the best way to ensure that your system will do what you want. Don't settle for general types of programs. If you ask a salesperson whether a computer will run a software package such as a word processor, he or she will say yes because virtually all computers will run some type of a word processor. But will it have the features you want? The best way to be sure is to decide which word processor fits your needs and then find a computer that runs it. If you can't find the exact package you want, at least have a list of the features you prefer and ask the salesperson if a word processor is available with those capabilities that will run on any of his or her computers. You should do this for *all* the software that you know you want, even if you do not intend to purchase some of it until later.

Second, if you know what software you will be using, you can select the computer **peripherals,** or attachments such as monitors and printers, with the features that you need. For example, if you are going to run financial packages, will you need graphics to display bar or line graphs? Will you need a color display? Will your printer need to produce letter quality print or graphics? Will you need a modem for telecommunications? Without prior knowledge of the programs and applications you are going to run on your system, you could make a serious mistake in your choice of these items by purchasing components with unnecessary or wrong features.

"Software first" is intended more as a rule of thumb than an inflexible edict. The software generally acts as a guideline to the selection of the hardware; however, there are exceptions. For example, you might require a specific brand or model of computer or certain types of components for a particular reason, such as gaining compatibility with a system at work or at school. In such cases the available selections will be more limited but not substantially restricted.

Step 5. Select Your Hardware

Once you have selected your software, you can begin your search for a system to handle it. Study advertisements, manufacturers' literature, and other sources. Or present your list to a local computer store salesperson and ask to see what is available that will meet your needs.

Keep in mind the additional software you may plan to purchase at a later time; your system should be able to run these packages as well—or at least have the expansion capability to do so. It is not necessary to purchase all hardware components together; you can delay the purchase of some optional items such as a modem or extra memory until you actually need them.

Step 6. Buy Intelligently

Do not buy the first computer you see, even if you think it's perfect for your needs. It could be you will choose that system, but as with most major purchases, the smart buyer takes the time to do some comparison shopping. Prices do vary from store to store depending to a great extent on the type of store and the services provided. There is also a significant price difference on some items depending on your location (such as urban or rural) or the area of the country in which you live.

No matter which computer system or accessories you think is best for you, some basic considerations should be kept in mind when shopping and making your decision. When looking at a system or individual product, ask yourself the following questions:

- Does the product meet your needs?
- Is there adequate expansion capability?
- Is the product well known and tested?
- Is sufficient documentation provided?
- Have you actually used the product?
- Have you talked with other users?
- Are you comfortable with the product?
- Have you thoroughly examined similar products?
- Is the cost within your budget?

If your answer to any of these questions is no, then you may not yet be ready to make your purchase.

The choice of where to buy your system can be as important as which system you buy. When shopping, ask yourself the following questions about the retail computer dealers you are considering:

- Do you trust this store?
- Are the salespeople knowledgeable, cooperative, and helpful?
- Is pre-purchase assistance freely given?
- Is post-purchase support provided?
- Is special training available?
- Is service or support available locally?
- Are service contracts available?
- Are prices competitive?
- Are prices clearly and freely stated?
- Are the products you want in stock?
- Has the store been in business very long?
- Does the store have a good reputation?
- Are references available?

When you have selected all the components of your system as well as what you consider the best place to make the purchase, stop and take one last look. Ask yourself the following questions:

- Do you know exactly what you're getting?
- Are you satisfied with your choices?
- Do you understand all costs?
- Are there any hidden costs?
- Will help be available should you need it?
- Do you have firm assurances of the delivery of any out-of-stock items?
- Will additional products be available if needed?

Again, if you cannot answer yes to all these questions, go back and re-examine the weak areas and see what you need to do to correct the problems. If you still have doubts, even at this late stage, do not be reluctant to seek additional advice from someone more experienced with computers.

Step 7. Use, Maintain, and Care for Your Investment

Most system hardware requires very little special care other than what common sense would dictate. Your software and the files you create need a little more care, but you will find this small investment in time well worth it in the long run. Unfortunately, once a problem with a computer makes itself known, it is often too late to do anything to prevent its recurrence. For this reason it is essential that you do the few small things for your system that under normal circumstances prolong its useful life, such as always replacing the dust covers when the system is not in use.

Take your time in preparing and looking, and be as sure and as well prepared as you possibly can be before actually making your purchase. If in doubt, wait. Something new that better suits your needs may become available, and if the current trends persist, prices are likely to go down rather than up; the cost of some systems has dropped by more than 50 percent over the last five years, while the overall capabilities have increased significantly. It is also possible that a particular item you want could drop out of the market, but a better, more powerful version is likely to replace it. If you take care in making your choices, you should be able to purchase a system that provides many years of service and enjoyment.

2

□ □ □ □ □

Learn What Is Available

Resources vary from region to region, but you should have access to most of them since many of the potential sources of information, such as magazines, books, and retail catalogs, have a national origin.

The various sources have been organized into three categories: (1) *General Product Information* lists those places you might consult to gain a basic idea of what is available as well as to search for more details on the items you like. (2) *Market Availability and Costs* refers to sources that are likely to provide information on current prices and the availability of the items you have selected as your preferred choices. (3) *Advanced, Special, and Hard-to-find Information* gives you some idea of where you might turn if the usual references fail to provide you with the data you need or if you have a special requirement.

This list is arranged on the premise that you will begin with a general source of information and then move to the more specific references to determine your individual system components before you search for firm prices. Most potential buyers have little or no need for the resources listed in the third group until after the sale, when they may want to join a computer club or user's group.

The diversity of available information can seem overwhelming. If you haven't already decided where to start, first talk with someone you know who has a computer. Then consider a magazine or two and visit a few local computer stores. If you don't yet know what to ask, tell the salesperson that you are gathering information and ask for some literature. A "game plan" will soon emerge in your mind, and you will develop an understanding of what type of system you want and what you want it to do. Keep careful written notes on anything you find of interest. Retain copies of articles, advertisements, and other literature that is helpful, and remember to make notes of specific features you found attractive about the product.

Carefully organize your research. You might use colored highlighters to mark specific parts of the literature that contain important information. A color-coding system might be very helpful. For example, you might mark things as follows:

Green	Required feature
Blue	Desired or optional feature
Yellow	Unnecessary or undesired feature
Pink	Cost acceptable
Orange	Compatibility confirmed

What to Look For

Always keep in mind that your primary objective is to design a whole system. It is not uncommon for someone to become so concerned about obtaining a particular component or feature that far more important features or capabilities are sacrificed, ignored, or lost in the battle to find little or insignificant ones.

You must be concerned about the *specifics* of each component, but only after you have satisfied yourself that it will work well with your potential system in a *general* way. Does it have the general features you want? If not, the specifics are irrelevant. For example, suppose you know that you will frequently need to produce huge amounts of printed materials and therefore will require a printer with a relatively fast print speed of at least 200 characters per second (cps). You may desire some other features such as different fonts, pitches, and enhancements, but still consider the speed to be your principal need. You should collect data only on printers with print speeds of about 200 cps or higher, and select a printer for your system that offers these features and compatibility.

Compatibility Possibly the most important key word to selecting and designing a successful computer system is *compatibility*. This does not mean that everything you have must be compatible, but it means that everything which operates at the same time must be.

Suppose you decide that you want to have a word processor, spreadsheet, data base manager, and graphics program on your system, but you will be running only one of these at a time. Your computer, its operating system, and your printer must work well with all of these software packages if you are to take full advantage of their features. However, since you do not plan to run more than one program at a time, it might be that these would not have to be compatible with one another. (Even though most microcomputers are single-task systems, some programs permit multitasking or running more than one program simultaneously.)

As you consider various components, check their features and specifications very carefully and verify that they satisfy the requirements of the other components you have previously selected. Be flexible. If you find something you really like but it does not seem to fit with an earlier product you had tentatively settled on, then you may want to reconsider the first item.

Capacity Capacity refers very generally to your computer system's ability to perform its functions adequately and is usually determined by the values of certain parameters or basic parts of the system. At some point you will be forced to make decisions about the capacity of your system. For example, you will have to decide on the amount of memory and disk storage space you need. You will have to choose from a number of different computers with various types of microprocessors and a wide range of performance capabilities. Similar decisions will have to be made about many of the other components of the system.

Sometimes these decisions will be made for you. You may have little choice concerning the amount of memory needed for your software. Or the program will not run unless you have a certain processor or type of graphics. However, in many cases you will have to make most of these choices on your own by carefully balancing your present needs, your anticipated future requirements, and your financial capabilities.

Options Options generally refer to capabilities above those minimally required for basic performance. There is not always a clear distinction between what is a basic capacity requirement and what is an option. In fact, these can change as you change your mind about what you want in a system.

Look carefully at the various options provided by your software and hardware. Often, a relatively simple addition can save you much in time or provide much in enjoyment. For example, if you will be using large or complex programs or working with large data files, you may find the extra cost of a hard disk well worth the savings in time, hassle, and storage problems you would expend in working with hundreds or even thousands of floppy disks. If you plan to work much with graphics, the addition of a color card and monitor would provide such a pleasing and often more visible display that you would probably find the extra investment well worth it.

Think carefully before simply rejecting anything outright. You should take care to consider your possible future needs when looking at options. Be certain that you have the capability to add them.

Level of Power   When you have gotten well into your study and have collected a substantial amount of data, you are likely to find that you have found several computers (or components) that would satisfy your needs but at various levels. You may have Computers A, B, C, D, E, and F (and maybe many more), all of which would meet your needs to varying degrees, with A being the least capable and F the most. Let's say that C hits the mark the best. While A and B are both lacking something, you could live with either, especially since they cost less. Computers D, E, and F all have desirable extras but cost more. Depending on your individual needs and financial situation, you would then have to select from this list.

Ideally, should one always select Computer C? Not necessarily. It might be that one of the more expensive models would provide for some future expansion or options that will make the system more usable and enjoyable for you. On the other hand, even if they are limited, it would be better for you to be able to get a somewhat restricted system such as A or B than to have to cancel your plans entirely because of financial difficulties.

You may very well find that you are faced with similar decisions for many of your system components as well. Decisions have to be made concerning the resolution of the graphics, the speed of a printer and the quality of the print it provides, the transmission rate of a modem, and features of various software packages. In Appendix B we will look at some of the ways to cut costs without compromising the system performance significantly.

Special Requirements   You may know from the very beginning of your search for a computer that you have some special or unusual requirements, but you may not discover until later that some of your needs are unique. In either case, as soon as you know about your exceptional needs you should begin to take these into consideration when selecting components and designing your system.

Relative Costs   Take care to remain very much aware of the relative costs of each component of your system. It is often the case that adding a single feature (even an inexpensive one) will require that other components be changed to accommodate this new capability, resulting in a considerable total system price increase. If the total cost begins to get out of hand, don't panic. Before you eliminate something that you really want or need, check to see if you can cut back in other areas.

General Product Information

These resources will provide you with a general overview of the computer world, what is available, and what the various components will do. After consulting some of these sources, you should be able to have a reasonably good idea of the features and capabilities that you might want in a computer.

Computer Stores   Most computer salespeople are more than willing to answer your questions and show you their systems in the hope of an eventual sale. Not only can you see computers demonstrated but also software packages that you might be considering. Nearly all dealers with demonstration systems permit you to sit down at the computer and try it out for yourself with a variety of programs.

There are several things to keep firmly in mind when reviewing a product at a retail store. The salespeople want to make a sale and are going to push their products. They are not likely to tell you about problems or weaknesses unless you specifically inquire about them—and maybe not even then. Also, you will see only a small selection of the available computers at most places, and a salesperson cannot be expected to tell you about the competition's systems. Unfortunately, some salespeople are not very informed about their products and can give you poor information or advice. (After a time you may actually find that you are more computer literate than many of those selling you computer equipment.) It is often a good idea to verify details with specification sheets from the manufacturer or some other source.

Magazines   The many magazines available that describe personal computer systems include reviews of new computers, accessories, and programs as well as retailers' and manufacturers' advertisements. Most also include articles on various parts of systems, such as memory, monitors, disk drives, and printers, which explain components and describe their features and how they function as well as what is new on the market. Until you have determined the specific brand or model that is best for you, you might prefer to stay with the more generic magazines that cover the most popular models. But there are also many publications dedicated to a particular type, brand, or even model of computer, and these may be attractive to you once you have a better idea of what you want.

Product Catalogs   Many special product catalogs are published each year that list nothing but computer products of a particular type. Some list computers while others provide a current roster for an accessory such as printers, modems, or monitors. Sometimes you may find several different components listed in the same source, but these lists are not usually as complete.

These catalogs are of two basic types. They may list only what is currently new on the market, such as hardware lists, which are part of a periodical or provided by consumer groups. The other type is a software catalog, which provides a more comprehensive list of what is available on the market and is distributed by private or independent organizations. You are more likely to find the hardware summaries on the newsstand near the end of the year. Check the major publications for special issues, reports, equipment summaries, or compendiums. These normally cost about the same as a regular magazine or perhaps more. While some descriptive material may be provided, most of these hardware lists have a brief summary of the technical specifications for each product along with the suggested selling price. Although brief, this is usually sufficient to provide a basis for some eliminations and further comparisons.

Software catalogs provide a brief description of the currently available programs for a specific type of computer or on a particular subject. Some of these catalogs are very extensive, with listings of many thousands of products. Software catalogs are available for most popular computers. Check with your local computer dealer or library for the availability of a catalog for any system that you might be considering. Software catalogs can be expensive, so you may want to review one before deciding whether or not to actually purchase it.

Catalogs are also published that list software by subject, such as educational programs and games. Also, some are dedicated to products that run under a particular type of operating system. If you have trouble finding a catalog of a specific type, check your library for catalogs that list catalogs. You should keep in mind that any of these catalogs will reflect a certain delay between the time it was written and when you read it, even the current issue. For this reason it may not include the newest products.

Reader's Service Cards   Many magazines contain special reader's service cards that permit its readers to obtain additional information on products described or advertised in that issue. Descriptive literature will be sent directly from the manufacturers.

Manufacturers' Literature   Aside from the reader's service cards, literature from manufacturers can be found in most computer stores as well as in many retail stores that have a large computer sales department. If you want more information on a product and cannot obtain it locally or through a reader's service card, you can always write directly to the manufacturer. The addresses and telephone numbers for many computer product companies are given in Appendix A. If you cannot locate a specific manufacturer there, the information can usually be obtained from any store that carries their product line. Also, some companies provide a toll-free 800 number for customer relations from which information can usually be requested. (Call the 800 information operators at 1-800-555-1212 to request a number.) You can also check an advertisement in a magazine for an address or telephone number.

When contacting a manufacturer, specify the exact models on which you want data and at what level you want the information—general and descriptive or specific and technical. Remember that information obtained directly from a manufacturer is designed as much for sales purposes as any advertisement in a magazine and should be treated as such; however, the brochures can provide information that may be hard to find locally or is more detailed and accurate than what is available elsewhere. They can also provide you with a good way to verify questionable information obtained elsewhere.

Performance Reports   Performance reports are useful for two reasons: They can give you valuable information on the technical performance of a particular product, and they usually provide data on how the product performs compared to other similar products as well as to industry or lab standards. Performance reports are available in many computer magazines and from many consumer groups. If you cannot find a report on a particular item in a recent issue of any publication, check annual or other indexes for a list of articles that have been published recently. If this also fails to provide the desired report, look for reports on a similar product. You may find the one that is of interest to you listed as one of the comparison products.

Be cautious, however, when reading such reports. Be aware of the source and satisfy yourself as to the objectivity of the report. Be certain that the authors and publishers have no ax to grind or product to push. You may encounter a publication that is not entirely objective. While it should not necessarily be avoided, the results quoted must be interpreted in the light of any possible political or economic bias that may have prejudiced the study. If you are uncertain about whether to trust the results of a report, look elsewhere.

Computer Shows   There is an increasing number of computer shows all over the country. These range from huge regional shows to tiny open houses sponsored by individual dealers. You would find it to your advantage to attend some of these. You will not only see many of the latest products, some of which have not been released for retail sale yet, but you will also have the opportunity to talk directly to the manufacturers' representatives and gather information and literature.

Check with some of your local computer stores about upcoming computer shows in your area. Ask about how to obtain tickets. If they can't provide them, they should be able to tell you where to write or call to request them. There is usually an admission fee to most of the larger shows, but you will find the experience and information gathered well worth it.

Books When you have a better idea of the type of system you want, you may wish to review one or more books written specifically for that computer. Books are available for most popular models that explain in detail how the system operates and what type of tasks it is best capable of handling. As with magazines, many such books can be found at your local library.

Market Availability and Costs

Aside from determining the components that will make up your system, you need to make several other decisions. You eventually have to decide if you want to purchase the entire computer system from the same place or collect individual parts from several different sources. In either case, however, you need to find out about the actual costs of all items as well as their market availability. How easy is it going to be to find the products you want at a price you can live with? There are clearly a number of places to look for this information. Where you will choose to look depends on your own personal preferences as well as what is available to you. If you live in a rural area with few computer stores, then you may prefer to rely more on mail order. On the other hand, if you are not comfortable with that approach, you may feel it worthwhile to visit one or more computer stores.

Buying Guides Several consumer buying guides are available during the year. These range from reviews and analyses by consumer groups to large volumes that survey the entire microcomputer industry in detail. Though buying guides can provide a bonanza of information as well as an excellent way to comparison-shop, some, especially the larger ones, can be very confusing to the beginner. Use these with care and only when you feel comfortable with the terminology used, and remember that sometimes a specification can be deceiving. Also remember to take into account the source and objectivity of buying guides.

Advertisements Consult advertisements in your local newspapers, magazines, radio and television, store windows, and even in direct market mail. You will find your best deal by knowing the market and doing a careful job of comparison shopping. You may run across a special sale or other great deal.

Retail Catalogs As a source of information do not ignore product catalogs, such as those from discount, department, electronics, computer, and specialty stores. These can provide you with realistic price quotations for your area as well as tell you where specific items can be found.

Retail Stores There are a number of different types of stores where you might look for a computer or some part of your system. These vary from full-service, dedicated computer dealers that offer a full range of computers and services to discount or mail-order stores that provide little more than a price, a box, and a bill. The choice of your retailer may be as significant as the choice of your computer.

In consulting sources for prices, you must be careful to distinguish between the *suggested retail price* and the *actual selling price.* It is not always easy to tell which price is being quoted. It may be that these two are the same, but in many cases the latter can be substantially lower than the former. Resources such as performance reports, buying guides, manufacturers' advertisements or literature, and product catalogs are more likely to list the manufacturer's suggested retail price. On the other hand, a dealer's advertisements, retail catalogs, and in-store prices generally reflect the actual selling price. Sometimes you will get lucky and both prices will be given for comparison.

If you cannot tell from the information given which price is being quoted, check before taking any action. Ask, if possible, and compare with other sources. It would be wise to avoid any dealers who quote prices that are very much out of line with the rest of the market, but be certain you are comparing similar kinds of retailers.

Advanced, Special, and Hard-to-Find Information

The following resources deal with special needs or unusual applications. They may not be as readily available or, in some cases, may not be free to you. Assess those you feel would be of the most help to you.

Computer Clubs and User's Groups There are many microcomputer clubs throughout the country. Some clubs are dedicated to a specific type or model of computer, while others are made up of members with a variety of systems. Most members of such clubs would be more than happy to answer your questions and discuss your needs with you. You might be able to attend a meeting and talk to several members to get more than one opinion. This may be especially helpful if the club represents many different computer systems. Check with your local schools (students are frequently members of such clubs) and computer dealers for possible clubs in your area.

User's groups are similar to computer clubs except that they frequently draw their membership from a wider geographical area, are dedicated to a single brand, model, or operating system, and offer their members (and sometimes others) special opportunities for acquiring software or other items. They can help you find additional information about the system they support as well as inform you about the availability of software. Some user's groups sponsor a buying club or other method through which its members can acquire current computer products at a discount price. Once you have decided on the computer you want, you might check with your local dealer for any local user's groups for that particular model. Computer clubs and user's groups sometimes advertise in the classified sections of computer magazines.

The membership lists of both computer clubs and user's groups are normally composed of people with a wide variety of backgrounds and capabilities. You will likely find some novice users like yourself as well as seasoned professionals. The computer club is more likely to provide you with a direct and personal learning experience with someone on a one-to-one basis, but you may find a wider data base of information to draw on from a user's group. Consider and investigate both possibilities and take advantage of one or both if you feel that doing so can be helpful to you.

Computer Professionals Most communities of any size have a number of computer professionals who are skilled at their work, ranging from programmers to systems analysts to college instructors. If you don't abuse the privilege, most professionals will be happy to take a few minutes to answer your questions and give you some advice. Your friends or the computer or data processing department at your company can provide leads. In the event that you cannot find someone on your own, here are some possibilities you might investigate.

An excellent but rarely used source of information is the student of computer studies. These students are usually very knowledgeable about microcomputers and the newest developments in personal computer systems, and most are eager to be of help. If there is a college in your area that offers computer studies, you might ask an instructor if one of the advanced students could be of help to you. Most instructors would be happy for their students to get the experience and would put you in touch with a capable student if one is available. Such students would help you gain a general knowledge and understanding of concepts, especially if you already know something about what you want and just need some technical details, and they could also be a real asset in helping you research the solution to any special need or application you have.

Other valuable resources are instructors at high schools, technical or vocational schools, and colleges; computer programmers; service technicians; sales representatives; computer buffs; or anyone else with a good working knowledge of computers. These people are often experts with one or more facets of microcomputers and can provide you with straight facts and also helpful hints you will not find in any published reference. In a few cases you might be able to get a demonstration or even some personal experience on a system.

If all your sources fail to give you the information you need, you might consider a professional consultant. For a fee, these knowledgeable people will assist you with your individual needs. If you decide to use a consultant, research your choice thoroughly before making any commitment. Also, since you will likely be charged an hourly or daily rate, be very specific with your requests so you will get what you want the first time.

Spotting Trends

It is difficult to determine what products will be the new industry pacesetters and which will lose out. Even the largest computer companies have had their failures. No matter how advanced or revolutionary a design, the only proven methods for evaluating a product are through direct marketing, consumer testing, and user reactions. There are, however, several ways that you as a future buyer can spot a potentially successful product.

Product Reviews   The product reviews in national computer magazines are usually objective and relatively thorough. These reviewers never say anything really negative about a product, but the absence of reviews for a major entry into the market may indicate a weak product or the presence of a problem that the reviewers do not wish to tackle. On the other hand, positive reviews are often routine for new products from major manufacturers but are not given as freely to lesser-known companies.

Consumer Reports   Product reports by consumer groups such as **Consumers Union** are likely to be more focused on user features and not as bogged down in technical details. Also, consumer reports tend to look more at the types of products or groups of products that are either already established or are beginning to increase their niche in the market significantly.

Response to Established Needs Look for products that are being offered in response to an established need. For example, 24-pin dot-matrix printers caught on very quickly despite their somewhat higher price because they offered letter quality print on a dot-matrix printer, which had been a need for many years.

Multiple Market Entries Experimental one-of-a-kind products are risky no matter how terrific they appear to be. Look for products that represent the flow of the technology in the particular area. It would be unwise to buy a computer with a new operating system or hardware design until you know that it will be supported by other hardware and software companies. Otherwise, you might find yourself with a computer and no software to run on it. Once several companies invest in the production of a specific technology, it is more likely to become successful.

3

□ □ □ □ □

Select Your Software

Software is a collective term for the **programs** or sets of instructions that make a computer function. Even the most expensive computer is no better than the programs that direct its actions. If the program contains errors, or **bugs,** then the computer will not properly process the data that is fed into it. Likewise, if the data that is entered into the system is incorrect, then the results cannot be correct either. (This is referred to by computer users as **GIGO**—garbage in, garbage out.)

Most software now requires a disk system of some type and a printer to take full advantage of its capabilities. When other special hardware is required such as a graphics board, this is noted in the discussion. (Refer to Appendix B for a software selection summary checklist.)

The Operating System

The computer's operating system is a set of programs that activates the computer when you first turn it on and permits you to perform certain basic and routine functions necessary for the operation of the system. It is normally (but not always) supplied with the computer when you purchase it, and you may need to know no more about it than what system and version you have. This is necessary because not all programs run on every version of a given operating system. Also, some computers support more than one operating system, and you may wish to acquire a second one to give you more versatility. If your computer has a disk drive (as nearly all do), the operating system will be referred to as the **disk operating system (DOS)** or sometimes the **basic disk operating system (BDOS).**

The **microprocessor** serves as your computer's brain. However, this brain "thinks" very differently. The operating system provides an **interface,** or method, for you to communicate with the computer, which includes all the necessary instructions you and the programs need to tell the microprocessor what operations you wish to perform. Without the operating system it would be extremely difficult to communicate with the computer.

An operating system is always written for a specific computer or group of computers. For example, **MS-DOS** works only on IBM-compatible computers. You interact with the operating system when you sit down at the keyboard and go to work. For this reason it is important to select an operating system that is comfortable for you.

Several types of operating systems offer various capabilities and features, and different ways for the user to interact with the computer. In addition, software programs are usually written for specific computers and operating systems. However, there are programs called **shells** and **emulators** that can simulate the operating system of one computer on another or make a relatively awkward operating system more user-friendly.

MS-DOS Versus Macintosh The two most popular computers in the home and small-business markets today are the IBM-compatible and the *Apple Macintosh* systems. Coincidentally, these two computers represent the opposite ends of the spectrum in the general design of operating systems. Here is a brief comparison of these two systems.

IBM-compatible computers, which use the MS-DOS (PC-DOS on IBM-made computers), rely primarily on direct keyboard entry and a command-oriented structure; that is, if you have a file named OLDFILE that you want to delete from your disk, you would simply enter DEL OLDFILE from the keyboard. Many commands are more complex than this, but the idea is basically the same.

Macintosh computers rely primarily on the use of screen **icons** and a **mouse** to enter commands. Icons are simply graphic images representing a particular item or idea. To delete OLDFILE on a Macintosh computer, you would use the mouse to locate the file on the screen and capture it with the button on the mouse. To delete the file you have just grabbed, you would move to the icon for delete (a trash can) and drop (delete) the file with the button.

Unless you have a reason for needing a particular type of system, you should try both in person before making a decision. Each has advantages and disadvantages. For example, if you plan to use graphics extensively, you may find the Macintosh preferable. However, this benefit is offset by the limited selection of peripherals such as printers. Also, the Macintosh comes with an excellent word processor and graphics program as part of its operating system, but you will find the market for additional programs more limited than that for MS-DOS-compatible systems.

If you like the user-friendliness of a Macintosh but must have an IBM-compatible for some reason, you might want to consider one of the many programs that can assist you with managing your DOS operations. These vary in type and capabilities and range from simple shells to full-system managers with many exotic features. However, most are **menu-driven,** and many include icons and permit the use of a mouse.

While the IBM-compatible and Macintosh systems are the leaders in the market, you may wish to consider several other computers. Commodore, Atari, and a few other companies have entries in the market that may be better suited to your needs. The Commodore and Atari machines are similar to the Macintosh, but many of the others are more powerful and expensive business-oriented models.

System Utilities   Most disk operating systems are accompanied by a set of utility programs that permit you to do certain housekeeping and disk maintenance chores such as copying, renaming, and deleting files; formatting, copying, and organizing disks; and checking on the contents, available space, and status of a disk. If you run only purchased programs on your system and do not do any development of your own, you may have only a limited need for many of these facilities. With time and experience, however, you will likely find them very useful. There are tutorials for most computers to help you learn how to use the system's utility programs.

Other System Software

A number of programs are available to help you enhance the performance of your computer. A few of the most popular and commonly available ones are listed below.

System Managers   While most system utilities are quite easy to learn how to use, a few are not. For these systems you can get a system management package that will do the most commonly used utility functions in a user-friendly manner. Most of these are menu-driven. Some of these packages are very simple and do only a few of the basic functions; others are complex and do almost everything for you, including controlling your entire system. These are priced from about $10 and up, with their capabilities roughly proportional to the price.

Shells Shells are menu-driven programs that are most often used as interfaces between the user and the operating system. They generally serve to make the present operating system more user-friendly and/or to simulate the environment of another operating system (that is, act as an emulator. See section on emulators that follows).

Copiers Many software packages are **copy-protected** and cannot be copied by the normal system utility copy program. In such cases you might try an independently written copying program that has been designed for your system. Such programs can successfully make copies of otherwise protected packages that are difficult to copy. You should be aware, however, that with the exception of public domain and shareware material (described later), the use of such copy programs to make any but backup copies for your own use is strictly forbidden by federal law. The license agreement that comes with your software usually gives information on copies that are permitted. Good copying programs are available for about $30.

Speed Utilities Some operations can take a relatively long time to execute. A variety of programs is available to accelerate systems in such circumstances. Some examples of such programs are speed loaders (to reduce the amount of time it takes a program to load into memory), disk cache programs (to increase the speed of disk operations), and memory managers (to optimize the use of main memory). Such programs are often found as part of a system manager and may best be purchased that way.

Print Spoolers A print spooler is used to permit the computer to continue with a printing operation while freeing the system for you to do something else. Spoolers, normally used with more powerful systems that have a hard disk, are found as part of the utilities that accompany many shells or other application programs such as word processors.

Emulators Some operating systems are more user-friendly than others. A few systems may offer emulators, which make one operating system look to the user as if it were another. For example, a microcomputer running under MS-DOS might be made to appear as if it were running the popular XENIX operating system. Terminal emulators are also available to make one computer or terminal respond like another.

General-Purpose Utilities

One problem with the operating system utilities is that they often are very difficult or awkward to use. Programs designed to replace the utilities singly or in part are fine but clearly limited in their use.

In recent years, a number of multipurpose programs have appeared on the market that perform most of the operating system utility functions as well as several other special and often very useful functions. These additional operations may include procedures that range from unerasing an accidentally erased file to rearranging the data on a disk to make the system operate faster.

Aside from the obvious advantage of performing many very useful operations, most of these packages are very user-friendly and make the routine operation and proper maintenance of the data on a system much easier to perform. However, they can be complex and take some time to learn, and some of the processes can involve an element of risk if not used properly.

Word Processors

Except for games, the most common use for personal computers is word processing. Word processing is much like typing with a regular typewriter except that what you type appears on the screen and is printed only after you issue a command. Errors can be corrected and changes made directly on the screen. Words, sentences, and entire paragraphs can be deleted, moved, and inserted as needed. Control over such things as margins; page length, breaks, and numbers; tabs; **headers** and **footers**; and general style (ragged or justified right margin) are frequently available. Many packages also permit highlights and special effects such as boldface, underline, italics, superscripts, and subscripts, as well as different type styles and sizes. You should take care to see that any printer you are considering supports the printing features of your word processor and provides a suitable quality print to meet your needs.

Some inexpensive word processors feature only a **line editor,** which means you may work on only one line at a time. If you need to work on a second line, you must move the text to align it with the edit line. The better packages offer a **full-screen editor,** which permits you to work at any position on the screen simply by moving the **cursor,** or position marker, to the location on the screen and then entering the appropriate commands or text. Although nearly all word processors now feature **word wrap** in which the text automatically continues on the next line without having to hit the Return key, a few very simple ones may not. Avoid these. Another valuable feature is automatic page breaks and page numbering.

Many word processors contain a spelling checker that finds and informs you of spelling errors. Some also have a thesaurus and a hyphenation dictionary, and a few simple grammar checkers are beginning to appear. Some of the more expensive word processors offer such features as automerging, which permits you to insert names and addresses in separate form letters and then print them without having to edit and print each one manually. Others offer indexing, which locates key terms and then generates an index. Others assist in the creation of outlines, tables, and figures, even permitting drawings and diagrams (graphics) to be incorporated directly into the text. These capabilities may come as part of the original package or may be available as an option.

Keyboard If one of your primary uses for a computer is word processing, you need to give careful consideration to the type of keyboard your system has. No computer keyboard is arranged or functions exactly like a typewriter, but some are closer than others. You will want to consider whether the keyboard is comfortable for you. Unless there is some very unusual feature, do not be too concerned with the arrangement of the keys; you will learn to adjust to this. More important is the presence of full-size and **full-stroke keys.**

Monitor Most serious word processing makes use of an 80-column-wide screen, which means that you may enter up to 80 characters on one line across the screen. Each character is fairly small and requires a sharp, steady image on the monitor screen. Many lower-priced color models give a very poor quality picture. The letters may be fuzzy or even wiggle. A **monochrome** (one-color) monitor works best for word processing on some computers. If you require a color monitor for other applications such as graphics and games, purchase a good high-resolution model. Also, many color monitors have a monochrome mode. Look at the monitor and use it with a word processor before purchasing it to be sure it is suitable for you.

Word-processor packages range in price from about $10 to several hundred dollars. Many of the professional programs offer special and advanced features that are valuable mainly to those who write complicated reports or prepare long manuscripts.

Desktop Publishers

If you are involved with the publication of a newsletter, newspaper, or any other printed material, desktop publishing may be for you. These programs provide the capability to produce camera-ready copy including large headlines, special type styles, pictorials, and other graphics, directly from your computer.

A few desktop publishers incorporate many of the basic features of word processors, such as text entry, editing, and perhaps even spell checking, but these products are generally aimed at a somewhat different end product. Most packages assume that the text has been prepared with an outside word processor and provide the capabilities for incorporating text or graphics files into a document and moving these files around as needed. They also normally include features that provide for special formatting of the output. This most often includes extended printer support for the graphics to produce large headlines, additional print fonts, extended character sets, columns, borders, and other special features needed to provide customized printouts. There may also be a collection of special graphics files called **clip art** that can be placed directly in a document and printed.

Although desktop publishers and word processors have traditionally been quite different and aimed at a different usage and user, this is slowly changing. Within the past few years, word processors have been gradually incorporating many of the special printing capabilities of desktop publishers, especially in the areas of clip art images and extended printer font support. Even though the desktop publishers have been somewhat more reluctant to increase their text processing capabilities, and the word processors are still far from the capabilities of desktop publishers, the trend is toward a merging of both categories of programs. Desktop publishers are presently priced with the upper end word processors.

Financial Software

Software is available to do almost anything in the financial area. Many small programs are designed to do only one job, such as balancing your checkbook, while others are comprehensive. Most programs do not require color monitors or graphics. They range in price from about $10 up.

Checking Account Programs   These are programs that keep track of your checking account transactions (checks, deposits, service charges, interest, and so forth) and automatically keep it up to date and balanced for you. These programs are usually inexpensive, simple, and easy to use.

Budget Planners   These programs permit you to plan and examine many possible budgets. Some packages may even indicate the best choice. As your finances change from month to month, the program automatically alters your budget for future months. This means that if you wish to make a purchase and pay it off in installments, you can enter the amount of the payments into the program, and it will indicate your new budget.

Financial Planners   This type of program is similar to a budget planner except that it is more comprehensive and usually permits you to develop a more detailed financial plan that may include long-term or anticipated items.

Assets Managers   Many packages have been written to assist you in keeping track of your personal assets. Some simply maintain an inventory list while others also allow you to include such things as bank accounts, investments, debts, assets, and income. Many also automatically factor in interest, dividends, depreciation, and other adjustments to your overall financial worth.

Financial Analyzers Analyzers permit you to make projections of possible financial situations and then factor these into your present and future budgets. For example, you might ask the program to determine the payments on a new car and then see how this would fit your budget. You could enter the prices of several models and more than one loan rate and time, if that is available to you. You would see which car, if any, you could best afford—or possibly even which would be the best deal in the long run.

Financial Managers This package may offer a combination of the above software plus such features as personal inventory, automatic depreciation, net worth, projected income, insurance analysis, and catastrophe control. These packages are often complex and more difficult to set up initially but are well worth the extra effort, especially if your financial situation is complicated. Some of the better programs even allow you to produce charts and graphs; these make use of graphics and possibly color. You will also find that managers tend to be somewhat more expensive, but the cost is less than buying the included programs individually.

Tax Preparers Up-to-date programs are available every year to assist you with your income tax preparation. These packages may even print the forms for you. The purchase price may exceed $50. You will need a new one every year, but most tax preparers charge you that much or more. Unfortunately, these programs are not written for all popular computers.

Spreadsheets

Spreadsheets are generalized financial management systems that are designed to be customized to your individual needs. You can use a good spreadsheet to do nearly any financial planning, analysis, or report required. They have a simple screen of rows and columns that you can set up to do the calculations and present the figures you need. The better packages can even construct graphs and charts based on the information you enter.

One significant advantage of spreadsheets is their power to project changes in a financial situation based on a set of numbers. Once you have defined your spreadsheet (which can be done directly on-screen with simple mathematical expressions), you can change some of your input data to see how it affects the end result. For example, if you have set up a screen to see how your retirement account might grow over the next 20 years, you can see instantly how it will change for different values of monthly contributions, inflation adjustments, and interest rates just by changing these values.

These programs range in price from about $10 to several hundred dollars. There are some relatively good and inexpensive packages but you may find them disappointing and lacking desired features. If you are interested in doing a number of financial applications on your system, you would likely find that the greater initial investment for a good spreadsheet will more than pay for itself in time. Those that produce graphs and charts make use of graphics and possibly color. Like a word processor, an 80-column screen is normally used, so either a monochrome or a high-resolution color monitor gives the best results.

Household Applications

You will find a variety of software designed to help you with nearly any aspect of daily life. The following is a list of just a few of the packages you might find of value. Color and graphics are usually not required. The cost may be as low as under $10.

Address Books   These are very simple programs that maintain a list of names, addresses, and telephone numbers. With these programs, information usually must be retrieved by name. However, a few of the better ones might permit you to retrieve by city, state, zip code, or even area code, giving you a list of only those people who live in a certain area. This could be of particular value if you have a very long list of names to handle.

Organizers   These programs will permit you to enter information for something such as recipes, records, tapes, tools, books, toys, collectibles, clothes, or even your computer software, organize this information in some way, and then retrieve it in some special ways. The retrieval of the information in an organizer is usually accomplished by the use of one or more identifying words or phrases.

One example of an organizer is a recipe file. With such an organizer, you enter all your recipes into the system then retrieve them by one or more key words or phrases. For example, you might request to see all your seafood recipes or maybe only those that use scallops. Some programs might even permit you to see all the recipes that make use of both chicken and onions and that can be prepared in less than 30 minutes.

Catalogs   Catalogs are a more sophisticated form of an organizer. These programs are intended for professional rather than casual applications. They generally offer more flexible retrieval capabilities with detailed cross-referencing of entries. Such packages are very useful for large collections of items such as coins, music, stamps, books, and cards.

Reminders   These are relatively simple programs that permit you to enter future events or appointments. Later, you can ask to see a schedule for the day, week, month, or even year. Reminders are often found as part of a larger program and may require or make use of a system clock, which automatically keeps track of the correct date and time.

Calendars   These are sophisticated reminders. They function not only as a reminder to inform you of your upcoming plans but usually include holiday notices. Calendars may also show you actual calendarlike screens with your schedule superimposed. These screens can be very helpful in planning events such as shopping, parties, vacations, household repairs, and so forth. While you can usually see any scheduling problem directly on the screen, some programs may alert you to possible or definite conflicts. Some of these programs employ color and graphics, and will likely require a system clock.

Project Managers   If you have many tasks to schedule in a short time or a high demand on a particular item, such as a car or a room, then you may need a project manager. These programs not only assist you in assigning times to events but also allow you to consider how long something will take and possibly even what materials or facilities it will require.

Video Production   These packages, which are very new to the market, permit you to convert your home videos into professional-looking productions with titles, subtitles, graphics, and even animations. Special hardware to interface with your VCR is required to run these packages.

Timers   Programs are available to permit your system to control certain external devices such as turning things on and off. These require a system clock and special hardware and wiring. Such packages can be fun, but the expense of the additional hardware is often not worth it unless you make extensive use of this application. Your money may be better spent on individual timers.

Security   Microcomputers can be set up to control your home security system. The same cautions mentioned above about extra items required for timers apply here as well. You should carefully study the economic practicality of this feature.

Data Base Managers

A data base manager (sometimes called an **electronic file cabinet**) may be the most powerful single software package you will encounter. A good data base management system **(DBMS)** can be a very effective and efficient organizer, catalog, calendar, and financial manager, and facilitate the orderly storage and handling of data. A DBMS is designed to be customized to your individual needs. Many are very powerful and can be amazingly versatile and creative in the ways they can be set up to manage specific applications.

The power of a good data base is its ability to retrieve information in a variety of ways. The output can be listed in a special order or to fit certain conditions. For example, you might ask for an alphabetical list of all names for people living in Ohio. However, the ability to get data out of a data base depends on how the data base was set up. Some data bases are much more flexible and easier to manage than others, and this should be a primary consideration when comparing these packages.

Data base managers vary greatly in price, ranging from about $10 to several hundred dollars. As with a word processor or spreadsheet, you would be well advised to invest carefully in a data base manager that will suit your needs. Very cheap versions are not powerful or versatile and may prove to be a disappointment. A package should be chosen wisely. Many data base management systems use color and graphics. Many require an 80-column screen.

Integrated Software

Integrated software packages combine the features of several types of software into a single package that offers you the capabilities of each individually. Although many different types of programs are found in an integrated package, the three most commonly incorporated in such software are word processors, spreadsheets, and data base managers.

One major advantage of this type of program is that information created by one section of the package can be referred to and used by another. For example, suppose that you need to include part of the information from the data base in a report that you are preparing using the word processor. With an integrated package, the information can be easily transferred. This type of cross-referencing compatibility is often lacking with software packages that are purchased separately.

Another advantage is price. You can get an integrated package for much less than what the individual parts cost when purchased separately and usually without sacrificing features or overall capabilities. However, integrated software packages range widely in price and what they will do. They can be found for as low as about $20 and cost as much as several hundred dollars for the top-of-the-line professional packages. As with any software of wide-ranging capability, the extra initial investment is usually well worth it.

If there is a disadvantage to integrated software, it is that you must take all three packages as a unit and therefore not have as much flexibility in selecting their individual features. To get a word processor that does all that you want it to do, for example, you may have to settle for a spreadsheet or data base manager that is not quite up to your preferred standards. Integrated packages may or may not make use of graphics or color but will likely require an 80-column display.

Telecommunications Software

The software that links your system to others is called a telecommunications (also **data communications**) package. These programs permit your computer to send and receive information from other computers over **data communications channels** such as telephone lines, microwaves, and communications satellites. You will obviously need access to a telephone line (or maybe just a jack) and a **modem** (which requires a **serial port** on your computer). A modem is a device that links a computer to a data communications channel, which for home systems is nearly always the telephone line. The telephone can be your regular home phone or an extension located at your computer. The expense of establishing telecommunications, including both the software and the modem, will likely cost between $100 and $500.

These packages can be used for many interesting things. If you have a friend with a personal computer similar to yours that also has a telecommunications program, the two of you can exchange messages, programs, data files, and other information over the telephone lines. You might transfer files directly from your computer at work to your home system, or students might send their homework directly to the computer at school. Your computer could even be set to answer the phone automatically and receive data from other computers even when you are not available.

Electronic Bulletin Boards One of the most popular uses of telecommunications is accessing electronic bulletin boards. These are computer systems that are accessible over the phone lines and provide some service or information. One common type is dedicated to a particular computer system and provides information to the users of that system. This may include information on new software or hardware products, comments from users on software or hardware currently in use, or even free software that you can **download** (copy) onto your system. Other bulletin boards provide more general information. Many also provide an **electronic mail** service that allows its users to leave messages for one another. Many bulletin boards are free, but there may be a long-distance charge.

Information Services There is an increasing number of electronic information services, some of which are local and others nationwide. These offer data bases that include information in such areas as current daily news summaries, stock quotations, catalogs, shopping (many types), education, health and medicine, literature, science, real estate, legal data, computer games, software markets, government, business, book and article reviews, weather reports, sports updates, traffic reports, and airline schedules. One service might give you access to well over 100 subjects. Many features such as games and airline schedules must be used while connected to the system; others, such as news summaries and reviews, can be downloaded to your system for later study at your convenience, saving connect-time charges.

Such services can be of real value and a lot of fun, but they can also be expensive. There is frequently a one-time subscription fee that may be as much as $100 or more plus a monthly charge that depends on how and how much you use the service. In addition, you may or may not have to make a long-distance call to access the information you want.

Graphics Programs

One of the fastest growing areas in personal computer software is that of graphics packages. Not only are these becoming much more reliable, versatile, and sophisticated, but the better graphics of the newer computers offer sharper pictures and new applications. In the past, games came to mind when people thought of computer graphics. While this was one of its primary uses for many years, it is rapidly changing. Excellent graphics packages are now available for many applications in education, engineering, art, drafting, business, word processing, and manufacturing. Many even come with a variety of ready-made images of geometric figures and other familiar objects that can be incorporated into your own designs.

If you anticipate the need to run any programs on your system that will make use of graphics, you must be certain that the computer has the appropriate capabilities to meet your needs. Most graphics software now makes use of moderate- to high-resolution graphics and probably employs color as well. Some may require special devices for input or cursor (screen position) control, which may include **joysticks,** a **mouse,** a **light pen,** or even a **tablet.** Check that your computer system can adequately handle all the graphics software you will need. Acceptable graphics packages are available from about $50 and up, which does not include the cost for any special equipment that may be needed.

Drawing Programs   These programs permit you to draw directly on the screen, usually by a special, manually controlled input device such as a mouse or a light pen. Some of these may permit very detailed drawings with variable-width lines and many colors.

Painting   Painting programs are similar to drawing packages except that they tend to be more "artistic" in nature. These usually permit varied types of brush strokes and a wide variety of colors (the **palette**). Often, a touch-sensitive pad called a **tablet** can be used to paint and transfer the image to the screen.

Sign Makers   Many relatively simple programs are now available to print signs, banners, posters, titles, headings, greeting cards, or other items requiring large or special print. (These may even be executed in color.) These programs usually work rather well, but obviously they require a printer capable of similar graphics. There are now variations of these packages designed to work with a word processor to enhance its printing capabilities.

Design Packages   This is basically professional-level software designed either to teach a field such as drafting or assist with design projects in industry. They normally require high-resolution graphics, often making use of three-dimensional displays, **plotters, scanners,** or other special equipment. Two of the most popular types of packages are **computer-aided design (CAD)** and **computer-aided manufacturing (CAM).** Not only are these packages widely used in education for instruction and simulations but also on the job in fields such as engineering, architecture, product testing, production, and tooling. Many CAD/CAM systems come as a unit with both the basic hardware and software, and may be very expensive.

Educational Programs

After games, educational software is probably the largest category, with good packages having been written early for virtually every personal computer system. Many of these programs make extensive use of color and graphics. Some employ joysticks, a mouse, a light pen, or even a tablet. Many programs also add sound effects or even speech, requiring a **voice synthesizer.** Educational packages can be found for less than $10, but some comprehensive programs can cost hundreds of dollars.

Drill and Practice   These programs are very simple in concept but tend to be dull, so they are often included with games to stimulate interest. Drill and practice packages offer repeated examples on a given subject for the student to answer and become more proficient in that field. Many provide automatic grading and review if the student does not do well. Some offer work on more than one topic or level.

Tutorials   Tutorials are designed to teach something, ranging from a single topic to an entire subject or course. They offer instruction on the subject followed by a test. Then, based on the results of your score on the test, you are directed to either review or go on to the next lesson.

Computer-Assisted Instruction (CAI)   Whereas drill and practice and tutorial packages can be used along with other material, most are designed to stand alone and be used without any other assistance. **CAI** software is more often used as part of a course to supplement the regular material. Many good CAI programs are available for personal computers to help you study and master new skills or learn new subjects.

Instructional   The above three categories all involve software that is designed to teach you something. Some programs, however, are intended simply to explain or show you how to do something. For example, there are packages available that explain how the system works, what it can do, and how to begin to operate it.

Preparatory   These packages are designed to assist you in preparing for some specific event. For example, there are programs that offer sample tests to help you study and prepare for certain national standardized tests such as the SAT and GRE.

Professional   Unlike all of the above, these packages are designed primarily for teachers and administrators. They are intended to assist with professional chores such as test writing, record-keeping, and grading.

Design   Many programs are now available for design projects ranging from art and drawing to drafting and engineering. These normally make use of graphics, color, and special input devices and can offer real versatility and creative expression.

Simulations   Many real-life situations, ranging from counseling to chemical reactions, have been simulated by a computer program. The student can then react to various sets of conditions and observe the results.

Games

Games probably comprise the single largest category of computer software, and there is a wide selection available for most computer systems. Most games packages range in price from about $5 to $50, with some very good programs available for $15 or less. A game often costs more if it is new or trendy, and it may become available later at a much reduced price.

If you plan to run many games on your computer, you will likely need a color monitor. Some systems function reasonably well with almost any monitor, but many require a good, high-resolution model to get a sharp image for games that employ greatly detailed or motion graphics. However, keep in mind your other needs, such as word processing. You may also need a set of joysticks to control the action on the screen.

Arcade   These are the familiar graphics action games that first come to mind when most people think of computer games. While many of these games are very repetitive and involve little thought, some demand subtle strategies that are not always apparent at first glance. All require graphics and most require color. Many need joysticks or are easier to play with them. Some people find these games the most relaxing type of all.

Adventure   These games lead you through an adventure the object of which is to find treasures or rescue a captive. There are normally many perils and pitfalls to impede your progress. Adventure games can be extremely challenging and rewarding when conquered. Most operate satisfactorily using a monochrome monitor, and most do not employ graphics.

Mystery   In this type of game you act as a detective or spy or other sleuth to try to solve a mystery. This may involve anything from a "whodunit" to recovering secret papers from the enemy. Some of these resemble adventure games in their plot, but they normally make more use of graphics and screen action.

Strategy   These may be based on almost any topic from sports to spies. You are asked to develop a strategy for the solution to a specified problem or set of problems. Many are similar to adventure and mystery games, but where these can be based to a great extent on trial and error, strategy games are usually more organized and less forgiving of mistakes.

Word   A word game may be an adventure, mystery, strategy, or other type, but it requires you to enter word commands to control the action. A key to the solution to the game may be the decoding of one or more clues hidden in a word or phrase. These games frequently do not use graphics.

Simulations   You are put into a real-life situation and asked to guide the action in a realistic manner. This might be an arcade-type presentation, such as the pilot of a jet fighter or an assault helicopter in combat. Or the setting may be historically based, with you as a general in charge of an army in the American Revolution or Civil War, with your results compared to the actual situations. While most of these games seem to involve a battle setting, some do not. Some might cast you as a race car driver, stockbroker, bobsled pilot, football coach, or even a doctor.

Game Shows   Several popular TV game shows are now available as computer games. These are close simulations of the actual TV show and should be a treat for those who follow these programs.

Sports   Nearly any sport that you can imagine from baseball and hockey to golf and skiing has been simulated for play on the computer. These popular games are available from several companies.

Card   Most popular card games, such as poker, bridge, and cribbage, have been programmed by several companies in various forms for the computer. Although these tend to be accurate representations of the games, they frequently lack imagination in play, and it is often not too hard to figure out how the computer "thinks" and learn to beat it most of the time.

Casino   These are similar to card games, but they simulate popular casino games, such as craps, blackjack, and roulette. These also tend not to be too imaginative.

Board   Nearly every popular board game has been programmed into a computer game, some more successfully than others. Many are offered by several companies, and some are only close clones. The computer tends to be "smarter" when you are playing against it in these games than in the card or casino games.

Number   If you like working with numbers then these are for you. They normally require the manipulation of one or more numbers to achieve a stated result.

Educational   It has been known almost from the beginning of computer use in educational applications that some students who resist the normal programmed instruction can be coaxed to learn when the lessons are presented as a game. For this reason much of the educational software is based on some sort of game to induce the student to learn. You can find games at all levels and on most subjects. In addition, some noneducational games, such as adventure, mystery, strategy, simulations, and even some arcade varieties, may be of value in teaching and developing logical reasoning and problem-solving skills. Games have been written that present almost any topic through high school level, including math, biology, history, grammar, social studies, spelling, chemistry, and literature. Most of these require the student to solve a problem or answer a question in order to proceed with the game. Rewards are often given for correct results and penalties for incorrect ones. The format may be presented either as tutorials or as drill and practice.

Business Packages

If you plan to use your computer system in your business, professional programs are already on the market to handle all aspects of the financial record-keeping, such as payroll, billing, sales, inventory, and so forth. There are software programs for pharmacies, farmers, doctors, churches, barbers, retail stores, schools, politicians, and almost everyone else. If a suitable package is not available for your unique needs, one could be specially written. An appropriate set of programs can be customized from a data base manager, spreadsheet, or integrated software package. Not all computers are suitable for this type of use.

Professional Software

Whatever your profession, it is likely that you can find software to assist you with your work. Several general application-type packages can be used for many on-the-job projects. We have mentioned professional-level packages for education and business applications as well as the CAD/CAM programs. There are many excellent professional-level packages for other fields as well. For example, there are Statistical Package for the Social Sciences (SPSS) and other statistical analysis programs, data and function plotters, report generators, equipment controllers, data analyzers, and many more. These programs are usually complex and powerful, and may be fairly expensive; they are not designed for the average user and do not work on many computers.

Programming Languages

All of the software discussed thus far involves pre-prepared programs that you purchase and execute on your computer. If you want to write programs for yourself, you need to acquire one or more programming languages. Capable and reliable versions of programming languages are expensive. You may expect to pay from around $100 to well over $1,000 depending on the specific language and its capabilities. Less expensive ones can be found, but you may find them disappointing.

Text Editors If you wish to get into program development, you need a text editor to write your programs. Text editors are very simple word processors designed for producing basic output files without special formats or control codes. They are frequently only line editors and may be both simple and awkward to use. They are usually included as part of the operating system utility package. They can also be purchased separately, or a word processor can be used, provided that it has a text editor or non-document mode.

Development and Run-time Systems Some languages come in two separate parts: the development and the run-time systems. The run-time system allows you to run only programs that have already been written. You must also have the development system in order to construct your own programs. Languages are sometimes offered this way to provide a less expensive package to those who do not plan to do any program development of their own. Because of its often high cost, this is frequently the case with the COBOL programming language.

Compilers and Interpreters You may also have a choice between a compiled and an interpreted version of a language. This is especially true for many versions of the BASIC programming language. Interpreters process a program line by line, interacting with and assisting you as you write the program. But they tend to be slow. Versions that employ a compiler are faster; however, you must construct the entire program (or an independent segment) and compile it to get any feedback. Interpreters are recommended for beginning programmers. If you desire, the programs that you write this way can always be compiled later, provided a compiler is available for your particular interpreter version.

BASIC This is the most commonly used language on microcomputers and is supplied with many systems. If it does not come with the initial system software, it should be available for your computer, probably in several versions. It was designed to be easy to learn and use by persons with little or no prior experience with computers and is probably the best language for the new programmer to learn first. You should not be deceived by the ease with which you can learn BASIC; it is a very powerful language that can be used to solve many complex problems.

COBOL was designed to be used specifically for programming business applications. It is a very complex and powerful language that requires a lot of memory and disk space to operate. For this reason it is not available for some systems; however, there are a few very good versions for the more professional computers. COBOL is not a difficult language, but it may be confusing for the beginner.

FORTRAN is a language oriented primarily for science, math, and engineering applications. It is not available for all computers. Although somewhat more complicated, the newer versions resemble BASIC in many ways.

Pascal This language was developed specifically to make use of structured or more ordered programming design. It is recommended by some as a first language because you are less likely to develop bad programming habits with it than with BASIC. It is more difficult to learn, however, and is not available for some computers.

LOGO is a very simple, conversational language designed for beginners. It is not a general-purpose language and is used primarily in education to teach children programming skills and problem-solving techniques. LOGO makes use of color and graphics and is available for most systems.

Assembly Language If you are very interested in program development, you may want to try programming in assembly language. These programs normally execute faster on the computer; however, they are very tedious and time-consuming to write. Unlike all the other high-level languages mentioned here, assembly languages are dependent on the computer in which they are intended to run.

This list is only representative and is far from complete. Additional languages, including Ada, ALGOL, APL, C, Forth, LISP, PILOT, PL/1, Prolog, RPG, and SNOBOL, may also be available for some microcomputers. Many languages come in several, often equally good but functionally different, versions.

Public Domain Software

Public domain software refers to programs that are not protected by copyright and are not restricted from duplication or distribution. Such software is normally available for roughly the cost of duplication. Collections are usually maintained by user groups and some dealers, and can often be found advertised in the classified sections of computer magazines. For some systems this can amount to many thousands of programs. In many cases the author is unknown. Public domain libraries tend to consist primarily of operating system utilities and games.

Most of the programs in public domain libraries are functional and perform a specific job, but some are not user-friendly or well written. Many assume that the user has a basic understanding of such things as operating system commands or the very process they are designed to accomplish. While they may not actually contain errors, they can lack the edit checks to catch improper entries that the better programs incorporate.

Shareware

The increasing complexity of programs has made commercial publication by the individual software author more difficult. However, with the proliferation of IBM compatibles, the number of such programs has become enormous. The immediate solution to this problem by the software authors has been the distribution of shareware or **user-supported** software. This concept was born in the idea that the users of a product will pay for and support it if they use it and find it of value.

Shareware authors protect their work by copyright but distribute their programs for little or no initial fee; they place few restrictions on the further distribution of the program by its end users. If there is an initial charge, it is nominal, usually about $1 to $7. Each program carries a message that if the user finds the program of value, the author requests a voluntary contribution of a certain amount, normally from $5 to $25. This can go much higher with the distribution of such material as the program source code, printed copies of manuals, hints to or solutions for games, templates, and other "special offers." Shareware programs can be freely copied or given away as long as they are kept in their entirety, and not sold or altered. Shareware programs range in value from almost useless to as good as their commercial counterparts; they tend to be better written than public domain material and are available for almost any job.

4

□ □ □ □ □

Select Your Hardware

Once you have a firm idea of what applications or specific software packages you want for your system, you are ready to look at the **hardware,** or physical equipment.

The variety of available products you will have to select from may vary significantly, depending on the basic systems that interest you. For example, the market is flooded with monitors, printers, and other devices for IBM-compatible computers, whereas the products from Apple are more proprietary in design and therefore your choices are more limited. This fact alone does not necessarily limit the performance of one computer relative to another and should not influence your final decision. (Refer to Appendix B for a hardware selection summary checklist.)

Compatibility

Compatibility is a key word in the selection of any computer system. There are several important considerations in this regard, some of which apply to nearly every system.

Software   The software and hardware must be compatible. Not only must the software be compatible with the computer itself (including the operating system), but it must also function properly with *all* other system components that it will use.

System   Many computers are designed to be compatible with and use the software designed for other brands. The most common examples are the *IBM PC* compatibles, which are supposed to run whatever runs on the corresponding IBM machines. To achieve compatibility, you must be certain that you are looking at a model that is compatible with the corresponding IBM machine, such as the XT, AT, or PS/2. While there may be some cross-compatibility, to select the wrong model will ensure trouble. Sometimes computers that are advertised as "compatible" are not 100 percent compatible, and a few are not even close to it. Some may also require expensive add-ons to achieve the compatibility that is claimed.

Plug Many independent companies make computer components, such as disk drives, monitors, printers, and modems, that are designed to work with certain popular computers by simply "plugging" the two together. These so-called plug-compatibles are supposed to plug directly into the computer and function properly. Note that some of these may not utilize all the features of your software, even when they have the desired features. This is not necessarily the fault of either the hardware or the software but rather a communications problem between the two. Such troubles frequently can be resolved by a **patch** or modification to your software program(s).

Other Standards Computers and system components subscribe to no universal standards, but several informally established norms may be important to you in selecting the parts of your system.

The Computer

The computer itself consists of several specific components. Some computers have only a processor and memory with a few expansion ports and slots, while others include such items as disk drives, tape backup units, graphics boards, a monitor, and maybe even a printer. Depending on what is included with the computer, the price could be as low as under $200 for a very simple model.

Here are some of the considerations you may encounter when comparing individual computers.

Processor The heart of any computer is the **microprocessor** or just **processor.** This is a **chip** or small but complex set of electronic circuits that controls the entire system and performs all the arithmetic and logical (comparison) operations needed to execute processing activities. A few computers even have more than one processor but use only one at a time for any given application.

A wide variety of processors is currently used in microcomputers, with new ones constantly appearing. Most are now **16-bit** models, but you may encounter one of the older **8-bit** or a new **32-bit** processor. Basically, this refers to the size of the block of data, or **word,** that the processor can handle at a time. The larger the word, the more data the computer can process in a single operation. This means that fewer operations are required with larger words to get a job done, and as a result it will be completed faster.

Another feature of processors you will likely encounter is the **clock speed.** This refers to how rapidly the processor can complete an operation or how many operations can be completed in a given unit of time. Most systems currently available run at rates from 1 to 25 megahertz (**MHz**), but you may find a few top-of-the-line machines that are faster. Clock speed may not be a primary consideration unless you plan to run software packages that process huge amounts of data, as many graphics design programs do. However, there may be better ways to achieve speed, such as through the use of a math coprocessor.

Some of the most popular microprocessors used with microcomputers are listed in the table below, along with some significant data about each. The values given for clock speed may vary with the manufacturer.

Popular Microprocessors Used in Personal Computers

Processor Chip	Word Size (Bits)	Typical Clock* Speed (MHz)	Commonly Used with
8088	16	8–12	MS-DOS
80286	16	10–16	MS-DOS OS/2
80386	32	10–25	MS-DOS OS/2
6502	8	1–4	Apple
68000	32	8	Macintosh
68030	32	16	Macintosh

*Rated clock speeds can vary significantly among systems.

Coprocessors A coprocessor is a supplemental processor that works to assist the main processor in performing specific types of operations. Coprocessors usually add to the abilities of the main processor rather than increase its speed, although the latter may be the apparent effect. One of the most common coprocessors is the math coprocessor (such as the 80287 chip) that works to increase the mathematical computing power of the main processor, usually by giving it the routines it needs to directly calculate values for various special, often advanced, mathematical functions.

Another type of coprocessor that is becoming very popular on top-of-the-line systems is one that handles operations through a high-speed cache memory (such as the 80385 chip), thus significantly increasing processing speed.

Memory is basically of two general types, **RAM (random-access memory)** and **ROM (read-only memory).** RAM refers to the memory that is available to the user to store programs and data. Information placed here can be modified at will but is lost when the system is turned off (or power is otherwise lost). ROM is preprogrammed memory that is available for use but cannot be changed by the user. Microprocessors, coprocessors, graphics cards, modems, and speech synthesizers are a few examples of devices that have ROM memory.

In microcomputers, the microprocessor contains only a few memory locations that are used for the temporary storage of program instructions or data as they are being processed. The **main memory** into which programs and data are loaded for processing is separate. This is RAM. It is normally measured in terms of **bytes,** or the amount of storage space required for one unit of storage such as for a single character. Memory is often referred to as so many K. While 1K = 1,024 bytes exactly, it is usually rounded off to 1,000 bytes. Thus a 512K system would have exactly 524,288 (512 × 1,024) or approximately 512,000 bytes of memory. One thousand bytes is also referred to as a **kilobyte** or **kB**, and 1 million bytes is called a **megabyte** or **MB**.

Most microcomputers come with a standard memory ranging from about 64K to 512K but are usually expandable to at least twice the basic value and often much more. This memory holds the operating system, the software programs that you are running, and the data to be processed. (A few computers have a ROM chip for permanent storage of the operating system, but most load it into memory from the disk each time the system is started.)

To get some idea of the amount of memory you need, look at the software packages you will be using and determine the *optimal* memory requirement. You may want to increase capacity. However, this value usually allows for ample data storage for the program to operate. If you will be working with large amounts of data or long files, you may wish to increase the memory. As an example, one single-spaced type page requires about 3K (in pica) or 3.5K (in elite) to store. Of course, the entire file does not have to be in memory at once, but it usually will process faster if it is. If you are in doubt about the amount of memory you will need, make your best guess but be sure you can add more later if you find you need it.

Boards contain electronic circuits either directly printed or otherwise mounted on them. A board that has other boards mounted on it is called a **motherboard.** A board that contains prongs or pins and is designed to plug directly into another board is frequently referred to as a **card.**

All of the circuitry in the computer and its peripherals is on boards in one way or another. This includes the processor, coprocessor, memory, graphics card, color card, ROM chips, and controllers. Even if you are not familiar with electronics or are not especially handy with your hands, you can probably install additional boards into your system if they are needed.

Graphics This relates to the ability of computers to generate and display noncharacter images such as pictures and drawings. Nearly all personal computers now support some type of graphics. Some come with the graphics built into the system, leaving you no choice about what you get. For example, Macintosh systems include high-resolution graphics that provide a sharp display. Others offer you a selection of graphics boards that can be installed. These usually include a good-resolution monochrome type as well as a moderate- to high-resolution color version.

IBM compatibles usually offer you a choice of graphics boards. You would be wise to select one that is considered as more or less standard and supported by the software you want. For *IBM PCs* or their compatibles, the **Hercules** and **MDPA** cards have been popular choices for monochrome graphics, while the **CGA** card has been widely used for color. The new **EGA** card supports more on-screen colors with a higher resolution display, and the **VGA** card provides an advanced, very high resolution output, but at a somewhat higher cost.

Color You may or may not need color capability. If you plan to do much that involves graphics, color can be very valuable, even essential. Also, for some routine applications the use of color for screen highlights can be interesting, exciting, and helpful. Determine your needs and be careful when selecting your monitor.

If a computer specifies that it supports color, check to see how many colors can be displayed at the same time. Some systems claim a **palette** of hundreds or thousands of colors and shades, but only a few of these can actually be used on the screen simultaneously.

Slots are positions in the computer for attaching more boards (cards) to increase or add to the capabilities of the system. They may increase the memory, add graphics, or attach a coprocessor. Slots sometimes are of different types (such as 16-bit or 32-bit). If you anticipate adding any boards in the future, be certain the computer has the slots for them.

Also, just because a computer is advertised as having, for example, six slots, this does not mean you will have six slots for additions at a later time.

Often, the basic computer requires some of the advertised slots for the memory, disk controller, and graphics card so you may have only three or four slots to use.

Ports are positions for attaching external devices such as printers, modems, and joysticks to the computer's processor. Ports come in a variety of types. There are those dedicated to a particular type of device such as a monitor or joystick, while others are more generic in nature. The general-purpose ports are normally divided into **serial** and **parallel,** according to the way they transmit signals.

Serial ports are used for modems and other input/output devices, while printers on IBM-compatible systems are most often connected through a parallel port. (If the printer is to be placed more than about 20 feet from the computer, a serial connection will be needed.) Apple and some other computer systems routinely use a serial port for the printer connection. As with slots, be certain that your computer has enough ports to satisfy present and future needs. (Unlike slots, additional ports can be added if you have a spare slot.)

Expansion Capability It is just as important to be certain that a computer has the expansion capability to meet your future needs as it is to verify that it will do what you want it to at the moment. Research the expansion potential of the computer with regard to total memory, disk storage, coprocessors, slots, ports, graphics and other boards, color, and upgrades.

Operating System The operating system used by a computer can affect its performance beyond how it interacts with the user. The more user-friendly an operating system, the larger and more complex it tends to be. This means it usually requires more memory and time to execute instructions. The result of this may be a slightly more sluggish performance and somewhat less memory available to you to run your programs. This can be seen with the Macintosh as compared to most MS-DOS systems. While the former are considered to be more user-friendly, they also tend to be slower and take up a larger percentage of the basic memory.

Data Storage

All systems come with some means of data entry other than the keyboard; these range from floppy disks to tape cassettes to cartridges. This is necessary because most of the software you purchase is in a form that cannot be read directly in order to enter it into the computer. The floppy disks and tape cassettes can also be used for data storage and retrieved at a later time.

Both floppy disks and tapes have a relatively small storage capacity, and the tapes are very slow. For this reason, larger hard disks are used for systems that need to retain a large amount of data. Rather than being removable and portable as floppy disks are, these are usually fixed in a sealed system and are referred to as fixed disks.

Floppy Disks   The most common type of data storage (and entry) system used on microcomputers is the floppy disk (also called **diskettes** and **flexible disks**). These single, flat, flexible plastic disks are coated with a magnetic material on which data is encoded and stored as magnetic signals arranged in concentric circles called **tracks.** These disks come in three sizes: 8-, 5¼-, and 3½-inch diameter. The 8-inch variety is no longer used on home systems, but both the 5¼- and 3½-inch are common.

The smaller diskette is not flexible like its bigger brothers but has a rigid case that serves as better protection from environmental damage. A typical 5¼-inch diskette can store from about one-third (360K) to just over 1 megabyte, while the smaller size can hold somewhat more. Even though there are a few physical differences between the two diskettes, they are used the same way.

Most software is supplied on floppy disks, so you will likely need at least one floppy disk drive for your system. These devices vary significantly in price but usually can be had for about $200 to $300. If you do not elect to have a hard disk, you should seriously consider a second floppy disk drive; this greatly simplifies the process of making backup copies (discussed in the next section). Most computers now provide for internally mounted drives, but external devices are also quite common.

Hard Disks   are similar in nature to floppy disks except that they are rigid and usually fixed and sealed in their mounts, they can store much more data, and they are considerably faster. They consist of a series of metal platters coated with a magnetic material for the recording of data.

Hard disks should be used with any system that will store a large number of files. They are also very convenient, since all active files are **online** and directly accessible without having to change and load from floppy disks. Until a few years ago, fixed disk systems were too costly except for the top-of-the-line models, but this is no longer the case. Computers containing both floppy and hard disk drives (up to about 20 megabytes) are now available for under $1,000, which is less than half of what a similar two-floppy system cost about five years ago. A 20-megabyte hard disk can be obtained in kit form for under $300.

Disks come in a variety of storage sizes beginning at 10 megabytes and going up to several hundred megabytes. There is no need to get the biggest disk you can find, but be very careful not to err on the other side either. Plan what you think you will need and then at least *triple* it; you will always need more space than you think (sometimes quite a lot more). Tripling the disk space will not triple the price; larger drives are not substantially more expensive than smaller ones. Other factors that affect the price of a drive include the **data transfer rate** and the **access time.** There are no set values for these two parameters, but the higher the transfer rate and the shorter the access time, the faster and more expensive the drive.

Most computer manufacturers offer hard disk drives to accompany their systems, but a number of independent companies also provide excellent drives. Many computers provide for a fixed drive to be internally mounted, but external drives can also be used. Also, some drives now come with a built-in tape backup system as either standard or optional for those who want an alternative to floppy disks for backup.

Tape Systems   Very few computers still use tape cassettes for data entry or storage, but you may encounter an older model that provides this option. These are essentially the same as audio cassettes (although high-quality data cassettes are available) and can be used for the permanent storage of data. However, few, if any, software companies still provide their products on cassettes.

Many of the early tape cassette data storage systems were much more unreliable than their disk counterparts and sometimes required several tries before a successful operation was achieved. Although the reliability of these units has been greatly improved, they still lack the flexibility and convenience of disks. Data recorded on cassettes is rigid and cannot be changed without rewriting the entire tape. Tape systems do provide, however, an excellent method for system backup.

Backup Systems

A backup system is basically a capability to make copies of any software (where the license agreement permits) or data files that you create. This is important because, like information stored on paper, the original files can be lost or damaged by unforeseen circumstances. A file backup method is recommended for any computer system and is essential for those that support a large or expensive program library or substantial amounts of data.

It is necessary to keep a current backup of as many of your system files as you can, but since only a few files will likely be changed or created between backups, you actually need to back up only the new or altered files. The types of backup systems are relatively limited but are normally adequate. Your choice will depend on several factors, such as how much and how often you use your computer, what you use it for, how much time you have to spend on backups, how much money you can afford for a backup system, and whether or not you have a hard disk.

Floppy Disks Floppy disks are a commonly used backup method. If your computer has only floppy disk drives, then you will likely use this method as a backup. It may also be your preference if you have a hard disk.

There are three basic advantages. First, you will already have a floppy drive for loading software onto your system, so no additional hardware would be required. Second, a single file or a group of files can be restored easily and quickly to the main disk. This means that if you need to replace some information on your hard disk from a backup diskette, you can select and read the files that you need. With a tape you would have to scroll through all the files that come before the one(s) you want. Finally, you can overwrite single files on a diskette without disturbing the other files, which is not possible with a tape system.

While floppy disks are faster and easier for working with a few files, they can be very time-consuming and expensive for mass storage. For example, to back up a 20-megabyte hard disk with 360-kilobyte floppy disks would take about 60 diskettes and several hours of work. This would also reflect a considerable investment in floppy disks to simply keep as backups, especially if you use the grandfather method, which requires that two sets of disks be used alternately.

Tape Systems Tape represents the two extremes in convenience and speed for backup systems. On the lower end, simple tape cassettes can be used to save and store files that are in the computer's main memory. If your computer uses a cassette system for data entry, you can load a program or data file from one cassette and then save a backup copy to a second cassette. While economical, this is a very slow method.

At the upper end are relatively fast **streamer** tape systems that use special tape cassettes or cartridges to store large amounts of data rapidly. The main advantage is speed. The entire 20-megabyte disk mentioned above could be saved to a streamer tape in just a few minutes. The disadvantages are cost and flexibility. Although the tape(s) needed to store the 20 megabytes will be less expensive than the diskettes, extra hardware is required to supply the tape system. Also, remember that files can be stored and retrieved from a tape only in a sequential manner. This means that the entire tape has to be read to get to a file near the end, and storing new files or updating old ones requires the creation of an all-new tape.

Keyboards

The keyboard is the one part of a computer system that is frequently over-looked or just accepted as coming with the computer. This should not be the case. The keyboard is the part of the system with which you will inter-act directly and constantly, and you should be comfortable with it. Check the keyboard of any computer to see if it is satisfactory for you. This could help you decide between models that are similar.

Do not necessarily eliminate a computer that you otherwise like sim-ply because you find difficulties with the keyboard. Most computers now come with a detachable keyboard. An increasing number of companies make separate keyboards, with some priced under $50. If you like a com-puter except for the keyboard, you might consider replacing it with the model you like better.

In general, examine the keyboard to be certain that it is well built and suits your needs, and you are comfortable with it. In addition, you should consider several other factors about keyboards.

Construction A well-constructed keyboard is essential if it is to receive much use. An inferior one will not withstand the many millions of keystrokes associated with heavy usage. Such keyboards may soon develop stuck, repeating, or otherwise malfunctioning keys.

Cord Check to see if the connecting cord is long enough to permit you to move the keyboard about for more comfortable usage. Some people like to rest the keyboard on their lap and sit back while entering data.

Touch Keyboards come with a variety of touches. The **full-stroke** type has keys—similar to those on an electric typewriter—that have a def-inite give and slight resistance when pressed. There is often an audible **key-click,** which may be turned off if desired. Full-stroke keyboards are now found on most computers and are normally preferred by professional users.

A few computers employ **limited-stroke** keys, which give only very slightly when pressed. These keyboards are similar to those found on many pocket calculators. It is also possible you will encounter a **touch-sensitive** keyboard, which has the keys printed on its surface and responds to a light pressure on the appropriate spot. These types of keys are generally not found on the more expensive or professional systems and are considered unsatisfactory for frequent use; however, you may occasionally find that some full-stroke keyboards have touch-sensitive pads for special input applications.

Key Arrangement Nearly all keyboards have the keys for the alphabet, ten digits, and the most commonly used punctuation marks placed in a standard typewriter arrangement. Not all typewriters are exactly the same in the arrangement of their keys, and neither are computer keyboards. If you are a touch typist or are accustomed to a particular key layout, you might want to consider a model with a similar arrangement. However, you will have several (perhaps many) keys on the computer keyboard that are not present on a typewriter, so some adjustment will be required for any layout.

Keypads In addition to the standard typewriter arrangement of keys, most keyboards offer one or more special groups of keys (keypads) for performing special functions. The most common types of keypads are the **numeric** and **cursor control.** A numeric keypad offers an arrangement of keys similar to that found on an adding machine. Numeric keypads are especially useful if you are entering large amounts of numeric data.

Cursor control keypads are used to move the cursor around on the screen and sometimes move about in a file. These always contain keys that move the cursor up, down, right, and left; however, they may also contain keys that do such things as clear the screen, move forward or backward in a file by a specific amount (such as one screen), perform simple editing functions, or jump to the beginning or end of the screen. This is a useful feature for many applications.

Most IBM-compatible computers come with both numeric and cursor control keypads. Some have one keypad that serves both functions. Macintosh computers do not have a cursor control keypad because they rely on the use of a mouse to perform these functions. Other computers vary in the design of their keyboards in this respect.

Function Keys Most keyboards have several keys that can be programmed to perform special functions. The number of such keys varies but may be as many as 12. Many function keys are capable of performing more than one task by using the Shift and similar keys. These keys are normally preprogrammed by the software package that makes use of them; however, some computers may permit these keys to be user-programmed directly from the keyboard.

Special Features Be on the alert for keyboards that offer special features. These may range from an extra key or two that perform useful functions to a touch-sensitive keypad that can serve multiple input duty. This is an especially important point to consider should you decide to buy a separate keyboard.

Monitors

A monitor is a device that accepts a video signal from a computer, converts it into an image, and displays that image on a screen. The idea is similar to television when it receives a broadcast signal from a local station or input from a cable company and converts it into an image that appears on the screen. A monitor, however, has no tuner to locate stations and is designed to process the input signals somewhat differently.

Since you will spend nearly all your time at the computer looking at the screen of a monitor, it is extremely important to choose the appropriate model. Many computer manufacturers offer a monitor with their systems, but a number of independent companies also make excellent products—sometimes at a substantially lower cost. Good monochrome monitors can be found for under $100. Color models start around $200, but an adequate graphics model could run twice that.

When looking for a monitor, keep in mind that you look at the screen of a computer monitor differently from the way you look at a television. When using a computer, you look intently at the image on the screen, whereas with TV your focus tends to wander. You should not select a monitor in the same way you would a television. View the monitors that interest you with applications that you intend to use on your computer.

Screens   There are three points you should consider about monitor screens in general. First, what size do you want? With a few exceptions, monitors come in screen sizes ranging from a mere 9 to a full 25 inches. The most commonly found sizes are 9 to 14 inches. A larger monitor will make the images larger but not necessarily sharper. To get sharper images you need a higher **resolution** monitor.

Second, a **flat-screen** monitor offers reduced screen reflections and glare, thus eliminating a substantial amount of eyestrain.

Finally, the most common display format is 24 or 25 lines of 80 characters each, but other formats are not uncommon. Lines of only 40 characters are used by a few computers with relatively low-resolution color graphics displays. While the shorter lines are adequate for games and many other uses, if you intend to do much work using a word processor or spreadsheet, you will want 80-column capability.

Monochrome   If you do not need color, a monochrome or one-color monitor is probably adequate. These monitors usually give good results for applications that require only text entry, such as word processors, spreadsheets, data base managers, financial helpers, and telecommunications packages. A monochrome monitor may be sufficient even if your needs involve some simple graphics. In general, monochrome monitors are sharper than equivalent color models for text displays and are less expensive.

For years there was only one choice in a monochrome monitor—green on black. Today, other colors are available. Amber on black has become popular in recent years. Although less often seen, monitors have also appeared that sport white, blue, yellow, and red on black screens. If you find a monitor that you like except for the color, ask if it comes with a different color phosphor.

Color   If you will be running a number of games or other programs that make use of graphics, you probably want to have a color monitor. A color monitor may cost you several times what a monochrome model would, but the use of the latter would sacrifice much of the pleasure and information supplied by color displays.

A color monitor can display only those colors your computer sends to it. You need a monitor that can interpret and display the output from the computer. If your computer is equipped with an EGA graphics board, then you want a monitor that is capable of displaying EGA graphics. However, to use a model with capabilities far beyond those of the computer is a waste. (Note: Many color monitors can be operated in a monochrome mode.)

Composite Versus RGB   The choice between a composite or RGB monitor may be automatic, since not all computers have video signal outputs for both. However, if this is a factor in your choice of a monitor, the basic difference between the two should be clearly understood.

Composite video is essentially the same as that used for ordinary television signals, whereas RGB uses a more precise control of color (red/green/blue) mixing and intensity that produces a sharper image. Color composite monitors are usually adequate for low-resolution graphics but not sharp enough for 80-column text displays. To have both a satisfactory image for word-processing-type work as well as good resolution graphics, you need an RGB monitor. RGB models cost more but are well worth it in the visual performance they deliver. (Note: Some monitors can process both composite and RGB inputs.)

Resolution   refers to the ability of a monitor (or other device) to produce a sharp image. For monitors this is usually expressed in terms of the number of *pixels,* or dots, that can be displayed on the screen. These dots are very tiny and make up images that are seen on the screen, but each

individual pixel is usually nearly imperceptible. Typical resolutions necessary for monitors used with graphics systems employed by popular microcomputers are shown in the following table. Of course, monitors with a
much higher resolution are available (for a much higher price) should you
need one. Don't select a monitor just because the numbers indicate that it
has adequate resolution. View it with some programs that require sharp
imagery and judge for yourself.

Typical Required Resolutions for Graphics Monitors Used with Personal Computers

Type of Graphics	Number of Pixels Horizontal	Vertical	Number of Colors
Monochrome			
Hercules	720	348	2
MDPA	720	350	2
Macintosh	512	342	2
Color			
CGA	640	200	4
EGA	640	350	16
VGA	640	480	16
Apple (double-high)	560	192	16

Persistence If you have problems finding a monitor on which the
image does not flicker, it may be that you need a long-persistence model.
This is a monitor that holds an image on the screen a little longer, thus
producing a more stable image. These will be slightly more costly.

From viewing your television, you know that voltage fluctuations in
the power line can cause the picture to jump. If the jitter is only slight or
intermittent, you might try checking another monitor of the same model
or examine it at another time or in another store. If the system is not protected from power line surges, test one that is or return to the store in the
evening, when power usage is decreased. However, remember that any
problems that you see now may reoccur later.

Graphics Most computers display graphics images differently from
the way they do text characters used for word processing, spreadsheets, and
similar programs. Basically, text characters are displayed by **block-
mapping,** which involves addressing an entire block of the screen at once.

With this method the computer can display only those characters that are stored in its video ROM. These are normally the standard 96 ASCII (American Standard Code for Information Interchange) text characters (similar to those on an electronic typewriter) and sometimes the extended set of fixed graphics images. On the other hand, graphics are usually displayed by **bit-mapping,** which addresses each individual dot on the screen.

One notable exception to this is the *Apple Macintosh,* which uses bit-mapping to produce all screen images. This gives you a virtually unlimited character set for display, but it also causes the operating system to be somewhat larger and slower than its MS-DOS counterpart.

If your computer will have graphics, you need a monitor that can satisfactorily display images. The basic considerations are color and resolution. Even if the match seems right, watch the monitor with several graphics packages to see if you are satisfied. A monitor may perform adequately with some types of graphics but not with others. For example, you may want more or less persistence to eliminate flicker or ghosting (afterimage) with motion graphics. The monitor must also be compatible with the computer's graphics system (Hercules, EGA, VGA, and so forth).

TVs as Monitors   If you cannot afford the entire system at once, you may be able to postpone the purchase of a monitor and temporarily use your present television for this purpose. This can be done with any TV by using an **RF modulator** to transmit the video signal from the computer to the antenna input of the TV. If you have a newer model television, it may be designed to function as a monitor and have a port for the video input. Some of these monitor/receivers are equipped to process RGB video input.

If you do not have a monitor/receiver with RGB capability, your TV will accept a composite signal. If your TV can function as a monitor, then it should provide you with the same performance as any composite monitor with a comparable resolution. If you use a TV with no monitor mode, however, you should expect the image to be a lower quality than a similar monitor.

Avoid monitors that have fuzzy or wavy displays. If you see lines across the screen, either fixed or rolling, this may be a sign of poor signal processing. The black on a good monitor will be sharp and deep. Be certain that the colors are pure and the images well defined. If it is a color monitor, check it in both the color and monochrome modes. Check the display for each of your major applications, especially word processing and graphics. However, always be certain that the monitor is in proper adjustment and that any problems cannot be corrected by the simple turn of a knob. Also, some apparent difficulties such as weak or limited colors may be the fault of the computer rather than the monitor.

Printers

You may find that the largest and most confusing component of your system to choose is the printer. Nearly all personal computer systems use **character printers,** which are printers that print one character at a time like a typewriter. Other types that print lines or pages are available, but they are out of the price range of most microcomputer system users.

Printers range in price from about $100 to many thousands of dollars. Aside from compatibility, you will be looking for adequate print quality, the features that you need or want, and a reasonable print speed. To get all three may cost more than you want or can afford to spend. Assess your priorities and see where you can compromise.

Many computer manufacturers make printers, but you should not ignore the many fine models available from other sources. Sometimes you can find a printer from one of the independent manufacturers that will be closer to what you want and at a lower cost. However, verify that it will be compatible with your computer and software. Some companies make models designed especially for certain computers, while models for other computers will have to be custom interfaced by your dealer.

Impact Versus Nonimpact   Impact printers are by far the most popular type used with personal computer systems. These printers make an image on the paper by physically striking the paper through the ribbon, much like a typewriter. Impact printers do not require special paper and offer the best selection of print quality, features, and speed for their price range. Nonimpact printers produce an image by a nonphysical means such as a thermal, electrostatic, or chemical interaction with the paper and the ink material. These printers are usually quieter than their impact counterparts, but they cannot make carbon copies, often require the use of a special type of paper, and may involve higher operating costs in other ways as well.

Print Quality   The appearance of the print produced by printers varies widely. Some inexpensive dot-matrix printers produce the traditional-looking "computer print" while others yield print that rivals the best electric typewriter. Laser printers can even produce "camera ready" output, including special print styles and graphics images, that appears as if it had come directly from a print shop.

A draft quality print should be sufficient if you use a printer only for rough drafts, informal reports or letters, and other work that does not require superior print. If you need to print formal letters or reports, you will want a printer that produces **near letter quality (NLQ)** or **letter quality (LQ)** print much like an electric typewriter. Printers that permit various special print effects are also available.

Printing Speed   Most printers have speeds from about 25 characters per second (**cps**) to around 400 cps. Many printers offer more than one speed, depending on the quality of the print that is being produced. In general, the better the print, the slower a printer will produce it. You can expect a printer to work in **correspondence** (NLQ or LQ) mode at about one-third to one-fourth its speed in **draft** mode. Thus, a printer with a draft speed of 240 cps will likely offer better quality print at about 60 to 80 cps.

The rated speed for a printer may not be the actual speed that you see in use. If a manufacturer rates a printer at 160 cps, this may not include such things as the time to advance the paper between lines, return the printhead, or print enhancements (boldface, italics, underline, and so forth). In reality, this might cause the 160 cps value to be more in the range of 120 to 140 cps.

Unless you anticipate having a very large amount of printing each day (say, hundreds of pages), you will find that the extra cost to get the higher print speeds may not be justified. If you will be printing only a few pages at a time or have larger printouts only occasionally, you should not find the slower speeds too inconvenient. Print speeds of under 200 cps (in the draft mode) are adequate for most users.

Print Buffers   All printers have a print buffer or temporary memory for the storage of data to be printed. If this buffer is sufficiently large, it can expedite printing jobs. Once the document to be printed has been received in its entirety by the printer, the computer will then be free for other tasks. If your word processor or other software does not have a print **spooler** (see Chapter 3), this can be a real time saver. Although it depends on what is being sent to the printer, a buffer of 8K should hold about three pages of information.

Dot-matrix Printers   are by far the most popular type of printer used by the personal computer owner because of their relatively low cost, adequate print quality, durability, and versatility. They form characters by selecting and printing the appropriate dots from a rectangular pattern called a **matrix.** Matrix arrays range from as little as 5 × 7 dots to as many as 24 × 36. The more dots used, the better quality the print; a printhead will usually produce more dots for LQ or NLQ characters than for draft mode print. The following is an example of a dot pattern using the six letters from the word MATRIX as they might be formed from a 7 × 9 array. Each * represents the dots that are used and each - those that are not.

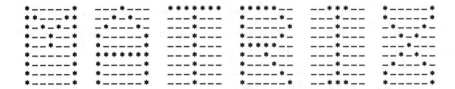

Although many nonimpact printers produce dot-matrix-style characters, the most commonly used method is by means of a **printhead** that consists of a series of small pins or wires that put the dots on the paper. For example, the above six letters might have been produced by a 9-pin printhead that strikes seven times for each character. If the number of pins is relatively small, then each dot tends to be distinct and the print undesirable. With a large number of tiny pins, the dots overlap and blend together. Many dot-matrix printers now use printheads with up to 24 pins to produce excellent LQ or NLQ print. Also, with a larger number of pins, the individual pins can be smaller so that each dot in the pattern is less distinct.

Many printers with 9-pin printheads can yield a fair NLQ font by using multiple passes of the printhead coupled with a slight shift in the position of the dots. In other words, in subsequent passes the dots are shifted vertically or horizontally by half the width of a dot. This means that a less expensive 9-pin dot-matrix printer can produce reasonably good print quality but at the cost of speed; the multiple passes cause the print speed to be reduced dramatically.

Some older or bargain-priced dot-matrix printers may be disappointing to you in more than just the overall print quality. Some models do not print true **descenders,** which are required for several lowercase letters such as *p* and *y* that extend below the line. Here is a comparison of a line printed with and without descenders.

With descenders: Now, jump quickly and be gone!

Without descenders: Now, jumP quicklY and be gone!

Such print may be acceptable if you do not plan to print very much in lowercase. However, it can be very annoying to read. Many professionals such as publishers discourage or reject this or any other type of poorly produced print, and you will likely find it unsatisfactory for any text-oriented uses such as word processing.

Variable Pitch Pitch refers to the number of characters that are printed per inch **(cpi)**. Standard pica is 10 cpi whereas elite is 12 cpi. Many printers offer a choice of several different pitches. Here are examples of several commonly available pitches.

```
This is 5 cpi.

This is 6 cpi.

This is 10 cpi (pica).

This is 12 cpi (elite).

This is 17 cpi (condensed).

This is 20 cpi (compressed).
```

It should be noted that **condensed** (or **compressed**) print is not always set at 17 cpi but commonly ranges from about 15 to 20 cpi. Notice that three of the sample pitches shown above represent double-width characters for three others.

Some printers allow you to mix pitches or set your own spacing. For example, you might be able to print with the smaller elite characters but maintain the pica spacing; this would have the effect of slightly increasing the spacing between adjacent letters. Many printers provide **proportional spacing,** which allots space to a character according to its width. This means that a narrow letter such as *I* or *l* will not occupy as much space as an *A* or *m*.

Standard spacing: `Mary had a little lamb.`

Proportional spacing: `Mary had a little lamb.`

This should not be confused with **microjustification,** which refers to providing even spacing between words in text that has blocked right-hand margins, as opposed to just adding extra spaces between the words.

Microjustified: It was one of those schizophrenic spring
                    days that seems unable to decide whether to
                    accept the rebirth of a new summer or to
                    hold on to the death of winter.

Not   It was one of those schizophrenic spring
microjustified: days that seems unable to decide whether to
                    accept the rebirth of a new summer or to
                    hold on to the death of winter.

The example of microjustification just given made use of what is called **justification,** which means that the right-hand margin is *justified right,* or blocked so that it is straight like the left-hand margin. Sometimes, it is desired to use a zigzag or nonjustified text, which is more like traditional typing. Then, the above example would look like this:

Not justified: It was one of those schizophrenic
                    spring days that seems unable to decide
                    whether to accept the rebirth of a new
                    summer or to hold on to the death of
                    winter.

Variable Fonts Font refers to the style of the print. For example, a simple printer might provide two fonts, one for draft mode and an NLQ style for correspondence mode. Many printers allow you to select more generalized styles such as block, script, and italics, while others even provide specific fonts such as Prestige, Courier, Roman, and Orator. Some even permit you to design and use your own customized fonts. Fonts may be built into the printer, available through cards, cartridges, or other plugins, or provided by programmed software as **downloadable** fonts. However, not all available fonts and pitches are interchangeable. For example, LQ or NLQ fonts may not print in a condensed pitch.

Downloadable Characters Printers with the capability to accept downloadable characters have an additional memory buffer to temporarily hold special characters that are sent to it from the computer. These may range from a single character, such as a letter of a foreign alphabet or a mathematical symbol, to an entire new font or alphabet.

Selection Mode The selection of a print pitch or font is usually simple when you can do it from the word processor or other program; this is referred to as being **software selectable.** However, there will likely be times when you want to use a particular pitch or font but you are not using a program that lets you designate it. Many printers have a control panel for this purpose that permits you to select your pitch or font mode directly. This is called **hardware selectable.**

Carriage Width Most printers come in one of two carriage widths: standard for paper widths up to 9½ inches and wide for paper up to 14⅞ inches wide. Before the various pitches were available, this was a relatively simple choice. If you needed more than 80 characters on a print line (pica was usually standard), you needed the wide carriage. Today, you can get the same number of characters on a line with a standard carriage by using a condensed print mode. The table that follows gives the number of characters that will fit on a line for both carriage widths for a number of commonly provided pitches. Other pitches may be available, especially as condensed print. Also, there may be a slight variation between wide carriage printers in the total number of characters that they will print on a line.

Number of Characters Printed per Line

Print Pitch (in cpi)	Carriage Width	
	Standard	Wide
5	40	68
6	48	81
7.5	60	102
8.5	68	115
10 (pica)	80	136
12 (elite)	96	163
15	120	204
17 (condensed)	136	231
20 (compressed)	160	272

Print Enhancements Most printers now provide some types of print enhancements. Commonly available enhancements include **bold-face,** *italics,* underlining, superscripts (such as $5x^2$ and $98.6°F$) and subscripts (such as H_2O and D_{max}), and overstrike (such as $\neq$ and fiancé). Usually most of these can be combined with one another or with the various pitches and fonts. For example, you might print $\mathit{STOP!}$ or $Co(NH_3)_6^{+3}$.

Color   Many printers now offer color capability. This may be a simple two- or three-color system that works from a single ribbon much like a typewriter that uses a multicolor ribbon. Others offer many colors, but the degree of manual assistance that is required varies.

Graphics   Most dot-matrix printers now offer some type of graphics capability. This is usually a **dot-addressable** method in which each dot in the matrix array can be individually printed. This means that the smaller the pin size (or the more pins in the array), the finer the detail of the image produced. Some printers can now produce graphics resolutions of several hundred dots per inch in which the dots blend together so well that the patterns appear to be solid and rival comparable images from plotters (which are discussed later in this chapter).

Tractor Versus Friction Feed   There are basically two ways to move paper through a printer: a tractor (or pin) feed for continuous forms and friction feed for separate pages. Nearly all printers provide for both methods; however, a tractor may not be standard equipment and may need to be purchased separately.

Most standard carriage printers have pins on either side of the platen that are used for pulling and guiding continuous forms through the printer. This type of paper is normally fed from either the rear or the bottom of the printer and continues through as you print. You then tear off what you have printed. Most people now use the **fan-fold** type, which is divided and folded by sheets, but roll paper works as well. A tractor is a device that has a series of pins for better paper feeding, but it can also be adjusted for different paper widths. A tractor is necessary for a wide carriage printer and is recommended for any printer when you have a large paper throughput.

If you will be using individual sheets, check the friction feed. Be sure that the paper feeds through easily and remains properly aligned. If you will be using both friction and tractor feed, check to see if feeding single sheets is possible without having to remove the tractor. Most printers permit you to use friction feed without having to remove the continuous forms. Friction feeding is slower (unless you have a sheet feeder described below) because you have to stop to insert each page, but this method permits you to use various paper types that are hard to find or unavailable as continuous forms. If you will use your printer for business, church, club, or other uses, you can print directly on letterhead or preprinted forms.

Sheet Feeders   If you plan to do a large quantity of printing using friction feed, you might want to consider a sheet feeder. These devices attach directly to the printer and feed the individual pages into the friction feed system of the printer. Sheet feeders can be found that feed one set of pages or more than one type of page plus envelopes. Sheet feeders can greatly speed up friction feed operations; however, they can be quite expensive (as much or more than the printer itself), are not available for all printers, do not function with all types of paper, and can be very temperamental to operate.

Ease of Use   Sometimes a printer that is excellent in every other way can make you wish you had a degree in engineering when you try to load the paper or change the ribbon. You might want to check on the ease of accomplishing these two tasks, especially if you are not mechanically inclined, before making a purchase.

Daisy-wheel Printers   Before the advent of dot-matrix printers that produced good quality print, the way to achieve true LQ print was with a daisy-wheel printer. Such a printer uses a **printwheel** called a **daisy-wheel** with a set of **fully formed** characters on it. This works much like the typing element of an electric typewriter by striking the paper through the ribbon to produce characters.

Such printers give excellent print quality, but they are slow, expensive, and do not offer the versatility of the new dot-matrix models. For example, while most daisy-wheel printers offer a choice of print fonts or pitches, to make a change in one or both of these normally requires that printing be stopped and the printwheel physically changed. Daisy-wheel printers are rapidly losing out to their more adaptable and less costly dot-matrix competitors.

Ink-jet Printers   are dot-matrix in nature but employ a series of tiny electrically charged particles of ink rather than having a printhead with a series of pins that physically strike the paper. Since ink-jet printers are non-impact, they are quiet to operate. The speed is comparable to a traditional dot-matrix printer, and the print quality is generally good to excellent. Some will require the use of special paper that is expensive and may not be aesthetically pleasing to you, but many of the new models can make use of standard paper. Some early technical problems have been more or less overcome so that ink-jet printers are now relatively reliable to operate.

Laser Printers   Rapidly growing in popularity is the laser printer, which produces an entire page of print at a time, much like a copy machine. These printers are fast, very versatile, and offer print styles and capabilities not found on other printers. They are expensive, however, and are not supported by all software packages. Please note that prices for some models are coming within reach of the home user.

Typewriters as Printers   If you have recently purchased an electric typewriter or plan to do so in the near future, you might check to see if the model will interface with a computer. Many modern typewriters can double as printers, and if the cost of buying the entire system at once is likely to be a problem for you, this could possibly permit you to postpone the purchase of a printer for a while. The use of a typewriter as a true letter quality printer could give you some additional flexibility in the choice of your regular system printer. However, while typewriters usually give very good print, they are normally relatively slow. Also, this may require the purchase and installation of a special interface for the typewriter, which can be costly.

Emulations   There is no universal standard among printers for the codes that are used to communicate with the computer. There are, however, several commonly accepted printer types that serve as unofficial standards and as emulation modes. These are often employed by printer manufacturers to increase the appeal, versatility, and compatibility of their products. Some of the most frequently encountered of these are IBM and Epson for dot-matrix printers, Diablo for daisy-wheel printers, and Hewlett-Packard for ink-jet and laser printers.

Modems

Modems are used to establish **telecommunications** links with other computers in order to access bulletin boards, electronic shopping catalogs, and public service information data banks. Most people visualize modems in the older **acoustic coupler** design where the telephone handset fit into a cradle on top of the modem (probably because this is the type most frequently pictured in movies and on TV). Today, modems may be in the form of a board that fits into a slot inside the computer; external modems are usually flat and about the size of a small book and connect directly to the telephone line. (Actually, the link can be over other **data communications channels** such as microwaves and communications satellites, but nearly all personal computer systems use a telephone link.)

As with most other computer equipment, the price of modems has come down significantly over the past few years. You can now get a model adequate for most home uses for under $100, but those that offer the most advanced and greatest choice of features can cost several times as much. With a wide choice of features and capabilities, modems are available from a number of companies. You should check to see if the systems that you intend to link with require any special **protocols** (the signals or commands needed to establish communications and transmit data) or other capabilities. You can then look for a modem (and telecommunications software) with these particular abilities. Otherwise, there are three basic areas that you will want to consider.

Transmission Rate This refers to how rapidly data is transmitted from one place to another. It is usually measured in **baud** or bits per second. For most systems this means that to transmit one character per second normally requires a rate of 10 baud. (It is 10 rather than 8 because there are usually 2 "control" bits transmitted with each character.) Common transmission speeds between microcomputers range from 300 to 9,600 baud. If you use the regular telephone lines, you probably want to use either 1,200 or 2,400 baud (300 baud would work, but it is very slow). The table that follows summarizes the transmission times required for the commonly used rates for sending or receiving one standard screenful of data. For the calculations that is assumed to be 24 lines of 80 characters each, or 1,920 characters (1.92K).

Data Transmission Times for Common Rates

Transmission Rate (in Baud)	Transmission Time for One Screen (1.92K) (in Seconds)
300	64
1,200	16
2,400	8
4,800	4
9,600	2

Most modems offer a selection of speeds. A somewhat greater initial investment for a model with a higher transmission rate may be more than offset by the eventual savings in long-distance charges when accessing other systems.

Auto Modes Nearly all modems now offer either or both **auto-answer** and **auto-dial (AA/AD)** capabilities. This means that the modem will answer any incoming calls to your system or permit you to dial a call directly from your computer without ever touching a telephone. Other models offer additional automatic modes such as automatic transmission rate selection. Your telecommunications software must also support these features.

Compatibility A modem must be compatible with the software that establishes the link as well as the communications protocols. There are several systems in use, but the most frequently used reference standard is that pioneered by Hayes. A **Hayes-compatible** modem should satisfy most needs, but you should check to see if you need any other special compatibility.

Other Input/Output Devices

Many other devices are used for data input, cursor control, and output of information.

Cartridges A few computers use cartridges for entering programs or memory expansion. Such cartridges are normally small units that simply plug into a special port on the computer. Cartridges usually interact directly with the microprocessor and require little or no preparation by the user. (Note: These should not be confused with tape cartridges that are frequently used as disk backup systems.)

Joysticks A joystick is a manual device used to control the cursor or some other screen motion by the back-and-forth, left-and-right movement of a vertical lever. There is usually a "fire" button to initiate certain types of screen action. Joysticks are most frequently used with games, but they have many other valuable uses that can add much pleasure and flexibility to the use of your system. Joysticks are inexpensive; good ones can sometimes be found for under $10.

Mouse A mouse is a small palm-sized device with a metal ball on its base. It is operated by moving it around on a flat, smooth surface; the motion of the ball indicates the direction, which is translated into the desired screen action. That is, move the mouse down or toward you, and the cursor on the screen moves down. As with a joystick, there are usually one or two buttons to initiate additional action such as capture and release. A mouse is most frequently used with graphics-based applications; however, because of their rapidly growing popularity, many types of programs are now providing mouse support. A mouse can be obtained for some computers for as little as $25, but the more popular models cost $100 or more.

Track Ball A track ball also uses a rolling ball to maneuver the cursor on the screen similar to the mouse; however, with the track ball, the ball rests on top of a fixed base and is moved with the fingers, the palm, a pencil eraser, or any other convenient method. As with the mouse, the movement of the ball will determine the action on the screen. Like a mouse, these devices are most often used with games, graphics, or other applications that require fine screen movements.

Light Pen A light pen consists of a light-sensitive stylus that is connected to the monitor by means of a cable. It can be used to enter, delete, change, or move values on the screen by simply touching it to the proper spot on the screen. These devices are most frequently employed with software packages that are to be utilized by a wide variety of users. They not only simplify the interaction with the system, but their use is much faster than traditional entry via a keyboard.

Tablet   A tablet is a touch-sensitive membrane connected to the computer for data input. A tablet is used by moving an instrument such as a pen (or perhaps even a finger) across the surface with a slight pressure. The tablet senses the position of the touch and transmits this to the computer. Although tablets are most frequently used for graphics applications, they can be used for other input tasks as well. If your computer has color capability, a tablet will permit you to take fuller advantage of this feature.

Scanner   Basically, a scanner is any device designed to scan and read printed, drawn, or other material. These range from relatively simple **optical mark readers (OMR),** which detect the presence or absence of a mark and are commonly used with standardized tests, to complex digital scanners **(digitizers),** which can read the fine details of engineering or other design diagrams. Also included in this category are **optical character readers (OCR),** which can read printed material, provided it is written in a font and size that the OCR is programmed to recognize. Depending on the capability, a scanner can cost up to several thousand dollars.

Voice Recognition   A few devices can interpret spoken commands and convert them into traditional computer input codes. Problems still exist with these units with regard to accents, homonyms, and other speech variations. Such units are still relatively primitive; have limited capability, vocabulary, and reliability; and carry substantial price tags.

Sound/Speech Synthesizers   Many computers and most monitors come with a speaker and limited sound output capability. If you wish to have more capability in this area than a particular system offers, you might want to consider a special sound synthesizer device. These units produce various sounds ranging from musical notes to a computer-generated imitation of the human voice. Some sound/speech synthesizers are internal boards that fit into a slot and others are external that plug into a port.

Plotters   Some of today's graphics printers are very good and produce high-quality images of pictures, graphs, and drawings that require fine detail. If you need more detail than you can get from even very tiny dots or you need a daisy-wheel-type printer plus high-resolution graphics, you might consider a plotter.

Plotters do not produce normal printed output but rather are designed to draw images with continuous lines. They come in a variety of designs including models that move the pens and those that move the paper. Color is more or less standard with most plotters; however, the degree of automation in its use varies widely. Plotters are available at prices that are competitive with the less expensive graphics printers, but the more sophisticated models cost several thousand dollars.

Protection and Convenience Devices

Several items that you might want to add to your system can provide both convenience for you and/or valuable protection for your equipment and data. In some cases the relatively modest investment can more than pay for itself in savings of time, annoyance, and repair costs.

Dust Covers   You would be wise to consider using dust covers for your computer and the other major components of your system, especially if they are placed in an environment where there is likely to be a high level of dust or other pollution. Covers can be found for most "standard" size components. These can sometimes be unreasonably expensive, and there is no reason why you cannot make your own from plastic or some other heavy, nonporous material.

Glare Screens   If you have to work in a room with bright lights that produce a glare on the monitor screen, you might ask about a glare-reduction device. These usually fit directly over the screen and reduce the reflected glare (as well as the screen intensity). They are available in most common screen sizes and cost from $20 to $50.

Monitor Turntables   Many monitors come with a turntable base that permits it to be tilted and rotated. This allows you to adjust the position of the screen for the best viewing angle for your height and sitting position. If the monitor you select is not equipped with a turntable, one can be found for standard-size monitors from most computer supply stores for about $25.

Printout Basket   If you will be producing long printouts, you might want a printout basket to give some order to the mess that can otherwise result. This simple device attaches to the rear of a printer and catches the paper as it comes through. They do not fit all printers and may not be usable at the same time with a sheet feeder or sound baffle.

Sound Baffle   This device simply fits over the top of the printer to reduce (but not eliminate) the noise. Baffles can get in the way sometimes, but some have access doors to help ease the inconvenience. They can be very expensive, so you might want to construct your own. Be sure not to interfere with the paper path, cables, or ventilation.

Static Guards One of the most common causes for data loss and even equipment damage is the static discharges that everyone has experienced in cooler weather. A touch to a computer or disk can result in a spark of static electricity that is fatal to data or a chip. Many products are available to help protect against such damage, ranging from mats to sprays, and are generally a relatively low-cost investment, considering the possible alternative. (These little sparks can also damage stereos, VCRs, and anything else that contains a microprocessor.)

Noise Filters Electrical disturbances called "noise" are always present in the AC power lines but are usually at such a low level that they are not noticeable. You have seen the effects of this noise as distortion in the television or radio; it usually appears as an audible hiss in the sound or flicker on the TV screen. Computers are just as vulnerable to this problem, only the effect is usually a loss or distortion of data.

There are devices that can be inserted between the computer and the power line that will filter out all but the most severe noise. They are not usually found as separate items but are most often incorporated into a power conditioner or other protective device as described below.

Surge Suppressors Another hazard with AC lines is voltage surges or spikes. Small voltage spikes are not uncommon and can occur whenever there is a disturbance along the power line. They can also damage data and, if large enough, your computer hardware as well. Nothing will protect against the massive surges that can result from a nearby lightning strike, but even simple voltage suppressors can eliminate most other spikes. These devices can be found as separate items or obtained as part of a more complex device offering more general protection.

Power Conditioners A power conditioner usually combines both surge and noise protection. They come in a variety of styles, ranging from a small unit that fits between the computer's power plug and the AC outlet, to large, multiplug models with complex switching arrangements. They cost from about $15 and up. (If a modem is part of your system, you would be wise to purchase a power conditioner that provides protection from surges along the telephone lines as well.)

Power Strips This is the familiar arrangement of usually four to eight electrical outlets in a strip. There is normally a master switch and a circuit breaker. Power strips may or may not be power conditioners. They are priced from about $10 and up.

Power Directors A power director is basically a power strip on which each outlet has its own switch. All of the components of a computer system can be plugged into such a device and each turned on or off using its switches. They start at about $50.

Uninterruptible Power Supplies   Most computers have a **volatile RAM,** which means that they will lose whatever is in their main memory should the electrical power be cut off. Under certain conditions a few systems can even experience more serious and permanent problems such as damage to the files on a diskette, possibly resulting in the loss of all the information on that diskette.

An uninterruptible power supply **(UPS)** is a power conditioner that contains a battery backup system so that it will cut in and supply power to your computer should the normal AC power be interrupted. These devices are not intended to run a computer for very long but are designed to provide power for a sufficient period to permit an orderly termination of any jobs and the shutdown of the system. The price of such a device will depend on the power output requirements and could run several hundred dollars. If you live in an area where the power is erratic, this could be a wise investment. After all, it takes only a blink of the power to clear the computer's memory.

Cables

The individual components of a computer system are connected together by cables. Sometimes the cables are permanently wired to one of the components, but more often this is not the case, and one or more ports are provided for this purpose. (Ports are female, and cable ends are male.)

There is a certain amount of standardization in cables and ports, but this does not prevent variety as well. You might encounter anything from the small, round RCA phono style or BNC coaxial design to the long, flat RS-232-C serial or Centronics parallel designs. Most computers have at least two or three different ports, thus requiring as many differing cable types. For example, the printer may use a Centronics port, the modem may need an RS-232-C port, and the monitor may make use of a D-style connector.

Individual components may not come with cables, in which case the proper cables may have to be purchased separately. In general, the type of port that the components will use for connection will determine the type of cable that will be needed.

Two components to be connected may not always use the same type of port. Also, if a cable has one end and a port is of a different type, it may be possible to find an adapter if the two designs are not too dissimilar. Finally, the length and quality of printer cables vary with the source, so this should be checked, along with the type and any special requirements. (More information on cables is provided in Chapter 6.)

Portables

An increasing number of portable computers currently on the market are **laptop** or briefcase size. These vary in their features and capabilities from those designed to function as a simple add-on to a fully operational system with a hard disk drive, built-in modem, and a battery pack for on-the-go operation.

Laptops may be the single most rapidly growing and evolving type of personal computer. For this reason a special appendix has been devoted to these machines. Appendix C is a reprint of a *Consumer Reports* product Ratings article on laptops that summarizes many of their features, advantages, and disadvantages.

Networks

A network consists of a group of computers connected together and organized in such a manner that they can share certain common facilities, including printers, disk storage units, data base managers, and other hardware and software components. The obvious advantage is that it permits each member of the network to have access to the common facilities without actually having to purchase additional ones. Of course, there may be a fee for this use, and a particular item such as a printer may not always be available when you need it.

There are many ways to organize a network. One of the most common for microcomputers is the **local area network** or **LAN.** This involves computers within a small area such as a room or building connected together with cables. LANs are often used in schools and businesses to avoid the duplication of less frequently used components such as printers and to permit access to a common storage unit. Other networks permit remote access using a modem. Some users find it to their advantage to either join an existing network or organize a new one in order to reduce overall system costs yet maintain or even increase capabilities.

Multiuser Systems

Nearly all personal computers are single-user models. Few people have the need for a computer that supports more than one user at a time. There are, however, several microcomputers that can and do support multiple users at once. This is usually done by the use of a **multitasking** approach, which divides the resources of the microprocessor among the users. A few systems have used **multiprocessing** by employing more than one microprocessor. The latter approach is losing out to the former due to the increasing power and lower cost of competing one-processor systems. (This may reverse again in the near future.)

Keep in mind that the number of users any multiuser system can adequately support depends not only on the number of ports provided but also on the applications to be run on the system. For example, a system can support more users doing relatively nonintensive tasks, such as word processing or program development with an interpreter, without a noticeable degradation in performance than users running very intensive tasks such as data base manipulations or running large language compilers.

Most multiuser microcomputers are not capable of handling more than a relatively limited number of users. Models that are powerful enough to adequately support more than a few users are normally very expensive. If you need to have more than one user with simultaneous access to the various components of your system, you might want to look into such options as networks and multiplexors before making a final decision.

Computer Furniture

There is an almost unlimited variety of styles and designs of computer furniture available. Some of these have been constructed to fit a particular model or type of computer, while others are modular in nature, allowing you to mix and match components to come up with the arrangement that best suits your individual needs.

Keep the following questions in mind when looking at computer furniture:

- Is it sturdy enough to hold all your equipment without any danger of falling?
- Is there adequate room for all parts of the system and still ample work space?
- Will the keyboard be at a comfortable height?
- Will the monitor screen be at eye level?
- Is adequate ventilation provided?
- Can you reach all components without unnecessary movement?
- Will the power switches be readily accessible?
- Is there ample storage space for manuals, supplies, diskettes, and tapes?

Computer furniture can cost several hundred dollars, which may be more than many parts of your system. Carefully research your choices. Sit at the desk (with a computer in place, if possible) and see how it fits you. Verify that the keyboard and monitor will be in comfortable locations and that the construction is rigid enough so that it will not collapse or topple over. Let the others who will be using the equipment try it out for their comfort as well.

5

□ □ □ □ □

Buy Intelligently

Where you buy something can be as important to a successful purchase as what you purchase. Be cautious and check out the store as thoroughly as the computer system. Before making any purchase, know the dealer's policies and reputation and feel good about the store.

Buying Software

When you buy a software package, read the features listed on the outside of the package and verify that they match your needs. Be certain that the program is written for your particular computer, operating system version, and system design, as applicable. What runs on an IBM compatible does not run on an *Apple Macintosh* and vice versa. If your computer supports more than one operating system or more than one version of the same operating system, check to see that the product is compatible with what you have. The description on the package will also give any special memory and disk requirements. Verify that this is satisfactory as well.

Version/Release Numbers   Software comes in more than one version. Version or release numbers are usually indicated as something like v2.3 or V4.21. These are normally preceded by the word *Release* or *Version* or perhaps only an abbreviation such as "Rel" or "Ver" or just "v" (or "V"), as used above. Release numbers are easy to interpret. The digit before the decimal indicates the number of the major version or revisions that have been released. The first digit after the decimal counts the minor revisions to the last major release. If there is a third digit, this indicates very minor corrections to the last minor revision. Thus, v2.3 would indicate the third revision of the second major release; v4.21 means that there has been one correction to the second version of the fourth major release. Finally, to confuse things a bit, you may find a package with *both* version and release numbers, such as Ver. 3.3 Rel. 1.3. The interpretation is the same as above. This would mean release 1.3 of version 3.3. (Note: Version and release numbers are not found on many games, one-time releases, or software for some types of computers or may appear in slightly different forms from the description here.)

The version of one package has nothing to do with that of another; you may have an operating system that is v4.0 and run a word processor that is v5.0. But you can know something about the product from the release number. A package with v1.0 means that this is the first version to be released and is more likely to contain bugs than one that carries a number of, say, v3.2. This is not to say that you should not purchase first releases; these have usually been well tested and are reliable. But given a choice, higher release numbers indicate more testing and actual user experience and feedback, which should improve the product. You would be well advised, however, to avoid anything with a number beginning with a 0, such as v0.2; these are often test packages and may not work well.

Registration Cards   Most software comes with a registration card or **license agreement** that you should complete and return as instructed. This permits the company that produced the package to inform you of any problem with their product and how to correct it. Most companies are willing to assist registered owners who have received a defective copy of a program. Many will also send you information on new and, it is hoped, improved versions of your software that you can order, often at a special reduced price since you already own an earlier release. Such offers are sometimes as low as 20–25 percent of the actual retail price. Finally, you may also receive information on other products offered by that company, sometimes with the option to buy at a reduced price. The license agreement also gives information about the actual ownership of the software (some software is leased rather than sold), any permissible copying, other legal uses of the software, and your legal rights.

Renting Software   Some companies rent software packages so you can test them before actually purchasing them. The rental fees are usually a fraction of the full purchase price, but you will likely have only a relatively short time to examine the package. If you do rent with the idea of possibly purchasing the material, ask if the rental fees apply to the purchase price. Also, you probably will receive a used copy for inspection; if you decide to purchase the software, return the used copy and ask for a replacement. This costs you more in shipping charges but carries a smaller risk of receiving a worn, defective, or incomplete package. Don't count on building up your software library by illegally copying rented packages; most are well protected and difficult to copy.

Buying Hardware

Although you should select your software first and then the hardware that can handle it, circumstances may dictate that the hardware will determine where you buy your basic system. A basic familiarity with hardware brand names leads people to look for hardware and then try to fit the software to it. Nearly everyone has heard of the most popular computers such as Apple, Atari, Commodore, IBM, and Tandy (Radio Shack), and possibly even some of the less well known but not necessarily any less capable brands and models, such as Amiga, AST, Compaq, Dell, and Zenith. Major software producers such as Ashton-Tate, Berkley, Digital Research, MicroPro, and Microsoft and popular software packages including Crosstalk, dBASE IV, Lotus 1-2-3, Symphony, and WordPerfect are probably less familiar to you because they are not as heavily advertised as the hardware and are less well known.

Tested and Name Brands Be cautious when it comes to products that are new to the market. This includes both computers and accessories that are either from a manufacturer who is just entering the computer business or represents a new concept or technology. Such equipment may be fine, but it will not have experienced the user testing of older models and may reflect a lower reliability. This is not necessarily the fault of the manufacturer. While most products are thoroughly tested before release, problems often are found only after actual use.

Many people are also more comfortable with a brand name that they recognize. You can often find as good or even better products from less well known companies, sometimes at substantially lower prices. You should not necessarily eliminate these from your choices, but if you do not know certain manufacturers, check to verify their reputation and determine how long they have been making microcomputers or accessories.

Beware of Unusually Low Prices Be careful of unusually low priced or vaguely described products. Some companies try to get the competitive edge on prices by removing certain standard accessories such as manuals, cables, or even the operating system, which they then offer to you at an additional cost as required extras. Beware of "quality" products. These may indeed be of fine quality, but they may also be cheap imitations. Unusually low prices may also indicate reconditioned or refurbished equipment, although such products may be fine, especially if they have been factory rebuilt and are backed by a warranty.

Used Equipment Be very cautious here. You might not be protected by a warranty, and you could end up with out-of-date equipment for which it is difficult to find software or service. Most computer stores do not deal in used systems, but a few may have a trade-in or demonstration model to sell as used or know of other customers who are ready to upgrade and need to sell their present system. If you buy a used system through a dealer, try to get the same warranty and benefits that come with a comparable new system. There is, however, a ready market for private sales between individuals.

Warranty Cards As with software, be certain to complete and return any registration or warranty cards that come with your hardware. (Some dealers will do this for you.) You should do this even if your system is to be serviced at your local store. You can never be sure when conditions will change. You may move to another city, or your local dealer could stop local service or go out of business entirely. Registration with the manufacturer and your sales receipts will help you verify your qualification for service under the warranty should it be needed.

Finally, look carefully at the manufacturer's product specifications. These are valuable when checking on the general capabilities of a given product as well as when comparing similar products. But take care; this can be tricky and deceiving. One printer may advertise a print speed of 120 cps while another claims only 60 cps. Are these for the same type of print? The latter could even be faster for your needs if it is for **correspondence** (near letter quality) mode while the former is for **draft** mode. Manufacturers rarely intentionally misrepresent their product specifications, but the wording can be misleading.

Buying Supplies

You will need printer paper, floppy disks, tapes, printer ribbons, storage units for your disks and tapes, and numerous other things for your system. There are many more sources for this material than for your hardware or software. You may wish to purchase your supplies from your dealer, but there is no good reason why you should not seek out the best buys for such items.

Wherever you purchase your supplies, be certain of two things: First, check to see that the specifications for an item match those suggested by the hardware or software. For example, if your computer's floppy disk drive uses double-sided, double-density (**DS/DD**) disks, be sure the disks you get are marked as such. Or when buying a printer ribbon, check both the brand and model number for a match.

Second, computer supplies can be deceiving. Very tiny differences in quality can make the difference between success and failure or a satisfactory or unsatisfactory job. Be careful about buying sensitive items such as disks and tapes that are either very inexpensive or manufactured by an unknown company. These items might be satisfactory for occasional backup work but may have a higher failure rate in heavy use. The quality of the paper or ribbon that you use could make a significant difference in the appearance of your printouts.

Types of Retailers

Several types of retailers offer a varying range of services and support both before and after a sale. In general, the number and variety of services offered is usually directly related to the prices charged; that is, the larger the discount, the fewer services will be available. But, there are considerations other than cost that may also be of concern in making your decision.

Full-Service   These stores offer a complete range of support and services for the systems they sell, including a well-trained and knowledgeable sales staff, the availability of special training, post-purchase support, and local service. All of these services may not be free with every purchase but can be obtained through the dealer, if needed. Many of these dealers will even deliver your new system to your home, set it up for you, and check it out to be sure that everything is working properly. However, some dealers claim to be full-service and charge accordingly but do not offer the corresponding services.

Full-service retailers tend to be the most expensive because of the extra services they provide to their customers. They normally charge the full manufacturer's suggested retail price, and with potential extra costs for training, support, or maintenance contracts, a total system cost can balloon significantly.

In this type of store you are most likely to get help in making your selections or be able to actually try out a system similar to one you might be considering. Full service is normally provided by most computer and some electronics stores. Some of these stores specialize in a certain type of system and do not offer a very wide variety of products to choose from.

Limited-Service   Here you will find some services available, such as a sales staff or service department. Training or post-purchase support is not offered. Prices may be slightly lower than at a full-service store because of the fewer services available, but often the services that have been eliminated are the ones that cost extra in the first place. Many electronics, some department, and a few discount stores are of this type.

Over-the-Counter   In this establishment you will simply buy whatever you want directly off the shelf without the benefit of a sales staff or a demonstration. Normally no extra services are offered including service after the sale, although most provide an exchange or sometimes even a refund for defective merchandise. The selection can be very good at some of these stores, especially for some types of software. Some department, most discount, and many mail-order stores are of this type.

No-Frills   Here you may not even have a store to browse through in making your selection. Most of these stores sell by mail and have little or no actual store in the traditional sense. You will likely get the best prices from these retailers, but you take the highest risk as well. The wide selection offered is extremely tempting to buyers who are looking for bargain or hard-to-find items.

Mail-Order   You will likely find the lowest prices through mail-order stores, but this could also be the highest-risk option as well. Not only do you risk an item being damaged in shipment, but there is also the problem of dealing with a seller by long distance. Should there be a problem with a product and you do not feel the store is treating you fairly, you do have certain very specific rights as a mail-order customer, but an uncooperative retailer can make life miserable until you force a resolution to the situation.

Direct from Manufacturer   Many companies sell their software or hardware directly, without going through a retailer. This does not necessarily get you a cheaper price; such sales are frequently at the product's suggested retail price. By ordering in this way, however, you may be able to obtain certain advantages that are not available from a retailer, such as a trial period. A small number of manufacturers such as Dell sell their products exclusively through direct-to-consumer sales.

Your Local Market

Your local market is likely to be very important to you in two ways: (1) It may be a very significant source of information as you are gathering data and deciding on a system. (2) Most people eventually purchase their equipment from a local dealer. The lure of the lower prices offered by mail-order companies entices many people away from their local market. Before taking this step, you should consider that in return for the reduced costs you may sacrifice some degree of support, carry-in service, or other benefits or conveniences that are provided by local stores.

There is generally a trade-off between services and price. If you want a fully staffed store that offers a wide range of support, then you are likely to have to pay extra for it. If you feel that you will need this type of assistance, then the extra cost may be worth it to you in the long run. If you tend to be a do-it-yourselfer, then you may be equally happy with an over-the-counter or no-frills dealer. Of course, you do not have to purchase everything from one source. You could very well purchase the hardware and basic software from a full-service store and some of your extras from a less expensive source. You could shop around and assemble your system from a variety of places to obtain the best value.

There is one very significant advantage in purchasing all the major components of your system from one dealer, especially if it is a complex system or one that you intend to expand. If one dealer sells you your entire system, then he *should* be able to ensure compatibility and service for the individual components. If you purchase a computer from one store and a printer from another, and then discover that they do not communicate properly, each store may very well blame the other and send you back and forth between them. Also, should you decide to expand or upgrade, your dealer should have a record of your system and be able to assist you so that you can maintain your system's integrity and internal compatibility.

If you go to a certain dealer to gather information and find the staff to be very helpful, straightforward, and honest, you might be well advised to consider that store for your purchases. Many buyers make the mistake of looking at the stores that provide information freely and then going down the street to buy their system from a discounter for a few dollars less. They later wonder why they have problems getting assistance or service when they need it.

This is neither fair to the first dealer nor is it very smart shopping. A store normally assists you in the hope of making a sale. Stores have no obligation to service or support systems purchased from another dealer and frequently do not. Even authorized factory service centers can and often do give priority to their own customers, and this is only fair. Remember the old saying, "You get what you pay for." Said another way, "You pay for what you get." The higher purchase price includes the pre-purchase support you have received as well as potential post-purchase support. If you have been satisfied with the help you have received, then you should reconsider before abandoning it to save a few dollars.

If you would like to deal with a local full-service dealer but cannot resist the temptation of the lower prices of a discount or mail-order store, ask your local proprietor if he would agree to cut his prices if you agree to waive some of the benefits that go with the sale such as support and training. You may find that some of the smaller, locally owned retailers are willing to deal in order to make a sale and boost their business.

There are now a number of nationwide chain stores that carry computer systems. These stores offer some advantages over locally owned dealers such as lower prices and a larger inventory. However, you may find that the local retailer is better equipped to provide the individual support and service you need. The chain store may be a more stable dealer, but the local retailer might be able to give you more personal attention.

Assessing the Need for Support

Even the most experienced computer user needs support at some time, which is one reason many companies provide telephone support lines. Before selecting a dealer, it is very important for you to consider carefully the level of post-purchase support you might need.

Some companies provide a minimum level of assistance free of charge; however, you may find that you have to pay a hefty amount for any intensive or extended support. Classes or other special training sessions are almost always at additional cost. If you decide that you want extended support, then carefully comparison-shop for that as well.

Do not forget to include your need for service in your considerations of support. Clearly, everyone wants to have service available, but there may be many levels of this as well, ranging from *shipping it back to the manufacturer* to *on-site service*. Again, the more convenience or support you receive, the likelier you are to pay for it.

Gathering Information

Research and gather information about the computer dealers that you are considering. When you visit a store or talk with a sales representative over the phone, consider the following points and make inquiries where necessary.

Helpfulness   Is the sales staff willing to assist you? Can they and do they answer your questions?

Demonstrations   Can you see and use a demonstration model of the system you want before actually making your purchase? This may not be as important when all components are supplied by the same manufacturer. However, compatibility is sometimes not universal, especially when brands are mixed and the system relies on so-called plug compatibility.

Competency Do you feel that the sales staff is well qualified and competent? Do you have confidence in what you are being told? If not, seek another opinion. It is a good idea to ensure that you will be satisfied with the service and support staff as well.

Competitiveness Are the prices competitive with other stores of a similar type? Don't avoid a local full-service dealer because he cannot meet the prices of a discount or mail-order store. A variation of a few dollars in the price of an item that may cost several hundred dollars should not be considered significant if all else is satisfactory.

Support Will the dealer provide support for your system should you need it after the sale? If so, is it free? If not, what are the rates and conditions? Exactly what does this support cover? It should cover everything you purchase from the dealer. If it does not, be careful; unsupported items can serve as a loophole to void or avoid support, or even service, for otherwise covered components.

If you are purchasing part or all of your system from a mail-order dealer or directly from the manufacturer, don't forget to check on any promised support from these companies. Don't assume that your worries are over just because you are provided with a toll-free telephone number to call in case of trouble.

Call the number. Do you get an answer? Do not assume just because the person on the other end of the phone represents a major company that he or she is accurate. You might be surprised to learn how much misinformation is given out by support personnel over these toll-free lines. This is probably not intentional but is because of inexperience or the inability to say, "I don't know, but I'll find out." When you call a number, try to have a few test questions to ask the person answering the phone.

Training If necessary, inquire about special training to learn how to operate your new system properly. Ask when it will be available and at what cost. Find out how many hours it will take and what it will cover.

Service Does the seller service all parts of your system after the sale? If not, where can you get service? Most modern microcomputers are vey reliable and usually operate for a long time (often years) between breakdowns, but should a problem occur, you don't want to have to ship a component to a service center in another city if you can avoid it. Some regional service centers are notorious for their long delays (sometimes months) in returning items.

Service Contracts   If you will have a complex or expensive system that will see heavy use, you *might* want to consider a service contract. In theory, service contracts are like insurance policies in that you pay a fee and then your system is fixed should it experience a failure. Such contracts frequently run about 10 percent or more of the total cost of the insured components per year. (Many dealers will issue contracts only on entire systems.)

If you think that such a contract might be for you, *be sure that you know exactly what you are getting.* Some contracts include *parts only* or apply to *carry-in service only.* Others may not apply unless the failure is of a certain type or from certain causes. Or, you may have to pay a large fee if no problem is found or if the difficulty is discovered to be because of your error in operating the system. Still others have tricky "void" clauses.

Service contracts are probably not a wise investment except possibly for those engaged in the most intensive and critical applications (such as in certain businesses), and then they should be entered into only with a company that has a good reputation and that has earned your confidence.

After the Purchase

Understand All Charges   Be sure to get an *itemized* bill that shows each item purchased along with its cost. Any charges for less tangible things, such as support, training, service contracts, shipping, processing, and taxes, should also be shown. Verify its accuracy before issuing any payments. Keep a copy of all sales transactions for future reference. If there is a problem or you have to make a claim for warranty service, then you may be asked to prove when and where you bought the item(s).

Know What to Expect   If you are to receive any post-purchase services, whether free or paid, be sure you understand when, where, how much, and to what extent each will be provided. This also applies if any part of your system is to be supplied at a later date.

Report Problems   At any time, especially within warranty periods, it is very important to report problems to your dealer or local service center as soon as you discover them. Most such places work from the date that the problem is reported rather than the date it actually occurred, if different.

Private Sales

A private sale from another individual can be especially valuable when you personally know or have the seller recommended to you by a friend. Also, if you need an item that is no longer available through retail stores, this may be your best or only way of finding it.

Almost everyone has participated in some sort of private sale transaction, yet the courts are jammed with cases involving misunderstandings. Here are a few simple guidelines for private sales.

- Exercise caution. If it doesn't "feel" right, leave it and move on to another seller.
- Ask why the item is for sale. Be sure that the reasons given are understandable.
- If it is a software package, do not accept a duplicate disk unless you know that it is public domain material. Selling duplicates of copyrighted software is against federal law, and you could become implicated should the seller be caught doing anything illegal.
- If it is a local sale, ask if you can see and check out the equipment. If it is a through-the-mail deal, insist on a ten-day return privilege. If either request is refused, you should proceed with extreme caution, if at all.
- The conditions of the sale, in writing, should include an exact statement of all provisions: what you will receive, what you will pay, any warranty or return privilege, the signatures (with addresses and phone numbers) of all involved parties, and the date.

If you are interested in this type of venture, you can consult the classified ads of your local newspapers for possible buys. Some national magazines such as *Computer Shopper* are also valuable sources of possible sellers.

6

□ □ □ □ □

Use, Maintain, and Care
for Your Investment

Most of what you should do to maintain your computer system and your data files in good condition is little more than common sense; however, computers do present a few unique needs and sensitivities that you should be aware of and understand.

Planning for Your System

Your computer and all of its components will need access to a reliable supply of electricity. If you use a multiplug power strip or conditioner, a single outlet is usually sufficient. However, this outlet should not be shared or on the same line with another electrical device, such as an air conditioner, refrigerator, electric dryer, or power tool, that draws a strong current. These devices can cause a significant variation in the output from a standard AC power line, especially as they start up. If you find this to be a consideration, a good, heavy-duty power conditioner should help to eliminate power fluctuations. (Most large computers in business and industry are placed on a separate, dedicated line to prevent any such interference.)

If you will be using a modem, you need to have a telephone jack nearby. If you will be transmitting a large amount of material by this method, you may want a separate line; otherwise you should be able to use an extension of your regular phone line. With auto-answer/auto-dial (AA/AD) modems, it is not necessary to have a telephone by the computer, although it is often convenient.

All printers make some noise, but some can be very distracting or disturbing. Under certain conditions, you might possibly run a long cable and place the printer in a secluded place, but this would not be very convenient for most uses. A better solution might be to use a sound baffle, a device that fits over the top of the printer and suppresses much (but not all) of the printing noise.

Personal computers do not require the rigorous environmental controls that their older and larger ancestors demanded. As a basic rule of thumb, if you are comfortable, your computer probably is as well. Extremes in temperature and humidity should be avoided whenever possible, but those maintained in most buildings are usually satisfactory. A much greater hazard is physical contamination. Besides dust, possibly the greatest potential gremlin for computer equipment is cigarette (or other) smoke.

Today, computers are generally very sturdy. Precaution and prevention are the best maintenance procedures. If you have several options for the placement of your computer, it would be wise to avoid rooms that have many open windows or an active fireplace. Try to locate your system away from windows or direct drafts. The continuous humidity from a large window, kitchen, or bathroom could eventually cause a problem, as could the airborne particles produced by food preparation. Finally, if possible, find a spot where the system can be permanently placed out of the usual traffic patterns in order to avoid any physical damage from its being accidentally bumped or knocked over.

Setting Up Your System

If you buy your computer system from a full-service store, it is possible that they will set up and test it for you. You may also receive training. However, an increasing number of people are buying their equipment from stores that offer a lower price and consequently fewer such services. You may find yourself with a number of boxes, manuals, and sometimes all-too-confusing and inadequate instructions. When you unpack, assemble, and test your system yourself, take your time and be orderly about it.

Unpacking As you open each box, remove the contents very carefully. Check all of the packing materials, especially any Styrofoam supports, for accessory items such as power cords, connecting cables (some components may have more than one of these), papers (such as warranties and supplemental or updated instructions), printer ribbons, demonstration or test diskettes, and small items such as extra fuses and screws. Many manufacturers are ingenious at concealing small but often vital components in the Styrofoam packing or hiding them in the bottom of the carton. Nothing is irreplaceable, but some items can take an annoyingly long time to get. It is not a bad idea to keep a list of what you find in each box for future reference in case of loss.

Inspection   Check everything very carefully for damage or defects. Internal damage within a box can occur during shipment even if there are no apparent external signs of mishandling.

Do not rely on an invoice, itemized sales receipt, or packing list to check for the completeness of the system. Consult the manuals that come with the components. These usually list the specific contents to be found, including all standard items but possibly not those that were added after the manual was printed, such as corrections or additions to the manual itself.

Do not discard the boxes and shipping materials. These are essential if you live in a rural area and need to ship a component to a service center. Even if your local store does this for you, it is still better to use the original cartons for shipment. Should you move, packing the computer system will be a concern, and these cartons will prove very convenient.

Cables   Your computer may come supplied with all the connecting cables you need, or your dealer may make them for you. If some or all the cables come with your system and you discover one is missing, damaged, or even too short, don't panic. Check with the store where you bought the system and see if they can help; in most cases they should be able to assist you. If that fails, you might contact the manufacturer and ask for a replacement. This could take some time.

If neither of these sources proves productive or practical, contact any local dealer who handles that model computer to see if they can provide a replacement. If that is not successful, any computer (and almost any electronics) store that has a service department should be able to make a new one for you. They will need to know the type of ports, pin configurations, and communications protocols, which should be in your manuals. If you cannot find the right information or are in doubt, bring the manuals for each component to be connected, and the service technician will do the rest.

Read the Manuals   Before you connect the various components together read your manuals. These will tell you exactly how and where to connect the various cables. There may also be certain DIP (described later in this chapter) or other switch settings that must be made before a component will function properly. Disks may need to be *formatted* or possibly *partitioned* before they can be used. Also, the operating system may have to be installed on the system. The instructions for all of these tasks are found in the system manuals.

You may wish to install auxiliary boards now, but if they are not essential to the operation of the system, it would be best to verify that the basic system functions properly first. Install the boards later and check each, one at a time. Should the problem be difficult to isolate, the fewer items you have to check and eliminate, the easier it will be for you to locate the offending component.

Assembly Once you are sure that each part of the system has been properly set up, you are ready to connect everything together. Check that each cable is plugged into the proper port and that it fits securely. If there are screws or clips to secure the connection, *use them.* Most components have a separate power cord. These should first be connected to the equipment and then plugged into the AC power outlet.

Testing Now you are ready to turn on each part of the system and see how it functions. If your computer comes with a special test or demonstration disk, that is a good place to begin. Otherwise, you need to use one or more of your software packages. It would probably be better to start with the simpler and easier packages to eliminate additional complications in case of a problem.

Check to see that each component of the system functions properly. In addition to verifying that all the hardware is in proper working order, you should also check to see that all software loads and runs properly. This does not mean that you need to verify the proper operation of every feature of every item; there will be time for that later. Perform basic checks to see that each component works in a general manner. If an item appears not to function, recheck everything and try again.

Report Damage If you find any damaged items or any that do not work properly even after going through all available checks and trouble-shooting procedures, report the problem immediately to the store where you bought the item. If you delay, it could adversely affect the action your retailer will take. Nearly any store will replace a damaged or defective item if it is reported promptly after the sale. However, if you wait weeks or months to inform the seller of the problem, he may then (with justification) decide to treat it as a breakdown that occurred after you received the item. In the case of software where there is no warranty or where the warranty has expired, you may have to replace or repair it at your own expense.

Start-up

Don't expect to do everything at once. *Take it slowly.* Learn the basics first so that you *understand* how your system operates. This way you will be better able to discover the cause of problems and resolve them. When the computer and all its parts are up and running, the operating system, the applications software you are using, and the printer or other additional components will be interacting together simultaneously. Sometimes the source of a problem is immediately clear, but other times it is very difficult for even a trained service technician to discover the offending part. The better you know your system, the easier it will be for you to diagnose problems and serve as your own service person, saving on unnecessary service charges.

Don't try to install or run all your application software at first. There will be ample time for that. Concentrate on one or two programs. You can then test each program in turn as you become comfortable with the ones you have tried. If you are not familiar with the computer's operating system, that should probably be the first task to tackle.

Start simply. Turn on only the computer. Study some of the operating system commands, such as how to list a directory or change from one drive to another. Read your manual. It will instruct you on the importance and procedure of making immediate backups of your system disks. You should do this *immediately* before doing any experimenting on your original disks. Once you are comfortable with the operating system, you can then begin to look at some of your other software. This one-step-at-a-time approach also applies to the hardware. The printer can wait until you know what you are doing with the computer and the software that will be addressing it.

System Boot A system boot is merely the process of bringing the system into a condition where it is ready for use. When you turn on the computer, it initiates what is known as a system boot. The computer reads from the disk and brings into memory the part of the operating system (the **bootstrap**) that is necessaary to make the system function. Please note that a few computers maintain their bootstrap internally on a **ROM** chip and boot without a disk. On most computers there are normally two ways to accomplish a boot: the **cold boot,** which is the type of boot that occurs when the computer is turned on from a power-off condition, and the **warm boot,** which is done while the computer is on. This can usually be accomplished directly from the keyboard or by using a special Reset button located somewhere on the computer. The latter is a nice convenience but is sometimes not effective in error conditions.

You may expect a pause between the time you first turn on the power and the time the system is actually ready to use. This pause depends on the system but is caused by several factors: If you have a hard disk, it has to be "brought up to speed" before it can be addressed. The computer has to load the bootstrap into memory. Most systems go through a series of self-tests and diagnostics before they release control to you. Finally, there is often a **batch file** (see following) that loads additional commands into memory.

A disk must be present in order to boot the system in nearly all computers. If you have a hard disk, this is usually automatic when you turn on the system. If you have only a floppy disk system (or wish to boot your hard disk system from a floppy), you must have a floppy disk in the drive and the drive door closed when you boot the system. Also, this disk *must* contain the bootstrap. Most application software does not come with the operating system already on it. In fact, there is often no room to add it. For this reason, if you will be booting from a floppy, you need to have handy *at least one* **boot diskette** that contains the operating bootstrap. You might wish to add to this disk any other operating system files that you find useful—such as those for formatting or copying disks; copying, renaming, or deleting files; checking the disk status; and so forth.

As your computer comes to life, it makes some noises that will soon become familiar to you. These beeps, whirs, and rumbles should not concern you unless one day you hear something unusual or clearly alarming. You will know that the boot process is complete when you see the **system prompt** on the screen. The nature of this prompt varies from one type of computer to another and may even be different for two computers of the same type if one has been customized by the dealer. But in general the prompt ranges from a simple symbol such as **A>** or **C>** to a full-screen **menu**. Once the prompt appears you are ready to proceed.

Batch Files   Many new computer users initially feel that batch files are only for computer experts and they are not likely to have much use for them. That is a misconception. Batch files are simple to write and can be helpful and convenient to even the most inexperienced user.

A batch file is a special type of file that causes one or more operations to be performed by the computer in a specified sequence. While there are times when a batch file is used to perform a single operation, normally it is used to do more than one. The procedure is simple. When the file is run, the computer executes the first job in the file. When that is completed, it returns to the batch file and executes the second job, and so forth until all the jobs in the file are completed. In this manner the computer can thus be instructed to perform a series of tasks without your having to be physically at the keyboard to type in each one as the preceding one is completed.

Batch files can usually be executed anytime the computer is operating. Probably the most common example is the file that is used to add instructions or programs to memory at the end of the boot procedure. This type of file is provided for nearly all types of computers; it is referred to as the AUTOEXEC.BAT file on an IBM-compatible system, and we will use that as an example.

Perhaps you wish to check (or possibly set) the time and date when your computer is turned on to ensure that they are correct. You can do this manually by typing DATE and TIME at the prompt. Let us assume you have three programs that increase the efficiency of your memory, disks, and printer operations, and you wish to load them into memory to make your system work faster. This might be done by typing MEMORY, CACHE, and SPOOLER at the prompt. Perhaps you have a shell program that shows you all the programs on your disk and assists you with routine operating system commands. We will call this SHELL. In order to accomplish all of this, you have to type all six commands *every* time you boot the computer. A batch file prevents you from having to do that repetitive task.

All you have to do is type the programs *once* into a file called AUTO-EXEC.BAT, as you would if you were doing it manually at the prompt. You can do this with any word processor that can create ASCII text files or a simple editor. The file would look something like this:

```
DATE
TIME
MEMORY
CACHE
SPOOLER
SHELL
```

If this file is placed on your boot disk (in the root directory), it will be run routinely every time the system is booted. These six commands are then executed for you automatically, and you never have to type the sequence again. The system will still pause for you to check and, if necessary, correct the date and time just as if you had entered these commands manually. You may, of course, change the file at any time.

Other batch files can be created and placed on any disk and named almost anything. The above is a very simple example of the real power of batch files. They can be made to pause for your instructions at various points or to accept variables such as file names, switches, or other parameters for processing. With some imagination and experience you can become proficient and creative with batch files and save yourself much time and many keystrokes. Refer to your operating system manual for details on writing batch files for your system.

Menus A menu on a computer is a list of what you may do under that particular program. Many application programs operate from menus. You may even elect to run your entire system from a **shell** program that permits you to control your system directly from menu options. You will often find that you have to move through several levels of menus before you get to the function you want. Opinions regarding the usefulness of menus vary, but the beginner normally finds them much more user-friendly and easier to use than trying to remember a series of individual commands.

Here is a simple example of a **menu-driven** program. You have an **integrated package** on your system that performs several different tasks. When you call up that program, it presents an initial list of the options available to you in the form of a menu that might look something like the following:

```
              GENERIC SOFTWARE

     A    Open a Document
     B    Create a Spreadsheet
     C    Enter a Data Base
     D    Make a Call
     E    Retrieve an Old File
     F    Import/Export Data
     G    Use File Utilities
     H    Exit to System

     Enter Letter of Selection: _
```

From this menu you can see the program functions that are available to you. All you do is select the letter (in other cases, the number) of the option that you want and enter it.

One of two things will then happen. Either you will be taken directly to that function and can begin your work, or you will be presented with a second menu. For example, if you select option B above, you would then see the traditional spreadsheet screen ready to receive data. In the case of Option E, you would be shown a list of the files that already exist and be asked which you wish to select. If you choose Option G, you would be presented with a second menu that lists the available file utilities. This second menu might look something like this:

```
        FILE UTILITIES

A  List Files
B  Copy a File
C  Rename a File
D  Delete a File
E  Return to Main Menu

Enter Letter of Selection: _
```

Clearly, menus could go through many levels, but if you find a program that goes beyond three levels, it is probably unnecessarily complex, and there is likely a better choice.

Some menus work a little differently. For example, a menu might make use of a highlighted bar that you can move along the option list using the arrow keys until you find the option you want. You can then indicate your choice by hitting the Enter (or Return) key. Other menus might make use of a split screen to offer more than one menu on the same screen or possibly a **window** to show useful information, possibly about your disk or the job you are currently doing. Still others may present a combination of these features or even more exotic display options. (Unfortunately, sometimes the most attractive thing about certain programs is their menus.) Become comfortable with menus—they are pervasive among software today.

Running a Program   To run a software program is usually a simple matter. If possible, select a program that does not require an installation or configuration program to be run beforehand. Installation and configuration programs are used to transfer copy-protected software to your hard disk and to make some special modifications to the program so that it will run properly on your system. Such programs are sometimes long and involved and would best be avoided until you are more experienced and confident with your computer.

Once you have selected a program to run, make a backup copy before you try to run it. Instructions for making a backup can be found in either your program manual or in your computer's operating system manual. When this is done, place the backup copy in the floppy disk drive. If you have a hard disk, you may want to go ahead and copy the program files to your hard disk. Otherwise, you can run it directly from the floppy.

A program can usually be run just by entering a single command or making a single entry from an operating system shell menu. You will then get the program's menu or request for a command. If it is a menu, you can probably make some sense of it. If it is a request for a command, you will surely have to look at the manual for help. But in any case, reading the manual is a good idea. You may want to experiment. However, if the program is complex or not very user-friendly, you will soon be leafing through the manual. (If you are in doubt, consult the disk label, disk directory, or manual for information on what to enter to start the program.)

You will find that many programs perform several different functions. You may not be interested in all of them. Explore the available options one at a time. Learn about what interests you the most and become comfortable with those features of the package, then go on to another program. You will have time to return later to explore the advanced and optional features when you have mastered your system and the basic operation of all your other software. This approach also allows you to test and become acquainted with as much of your software as possible in the least amount of time.

Help Menus Many programs now offer on-screen **help menus** that provide varying degrees of assistance directly on the screen by just hitting a certain key. This is usually in the form of a menu that appears somewhere on the screen until you hit another key to make it disappear. The amount of help varies with the program: It can be minimal and almost useless, or excellent and nearly as good as the manual itself. Also, such help may be available only at certain points in the program or may be found at nearly any time. Always check for it; it can be invaluable if available.

Troubleshooting Hardware Problems

If your system is all set up and ready to go but you find that part or all of it doesn't work, don't panic and call for help (especially if you will be charged for it) until you first check out a few simple things. The problem may be a loose connection or another simple oversight that is easy for you to correct once you locate it. Any experienced service technician can relate stories of systems that were "down" because a cable was loose or the power plug was disconnected. Service contracts or warranties do not cover problems that result from user carelessness.

Some situations may become apparent only with the use of the system; you should always be alert for any unusual, erratic, or poor performance by any part of the system and check it out immediately. Many of the manuals that accompany the hardware and software items offer suggestions for troubleshooting their particular products. Here are some additional guidelines.

Isolate the Problem   If at least part of the system works, then the first thing you should do is try to isolate the problem to a particular component. This will greatly simplify your troubleshooting tasks.

Power Plugs   Be sure that all power cords are securely plugged into the power line and firmly attached to their respective component. In the latter case, sometimes the cords require a little extra push to become properly seated and make contact.

On/Off Switches   Check that everything is turned on. Verify not only that the individual components are turned on but that the switches on any power strips or conditioners are on as well. Many devices have a "power on" indicator light, and a few even beep when turned on. If in doubt, turn a component off and then back on (remembering to wait a few seconds in between).

Fuses and Breakers   If all plugs and switches check out but there is still no sign of power, check for loose or bad fuses or thrown circuit breakers. These are found on most individual components as well as on all good power strips and conditioners. If after replacing or resetting an offending fuse or breaker it continues to fail, do not persist; there may be a short somewhere. If the problem is with an item of equipment, then it may be defective. If a power strip or conditioner is the problem, then possibly you are overloading it. Check the sum of the rated power requirements of all items plugged into it against its rated capacity.

Proper Mode   Many components have one or more mode selection switches, buttons, or other controls. For example, most printers have an Online/Offline indicator that must show Online in order for it to receive data for printing. Verify that the proper modes are set.

Drive Doors   If you are using a floppy disk drive, be certain that the drive door is closed when it is in use; it will not function otherwise.

Connectors and Pins   Check all connecting cables to be certain they are plugged into the correct ports and the connections are secure. You should be able to feel the cable slip into the port. Use the little screws or clips when available to secure the cables in place. If you are using RS-232-C or another type of connector that employs pins at the ends of the cables, check to see if any of the pins are bent or broken. Match the pattern against the one shown in the manuals to see if any pins are missing or possibly in the wrong position.

Hardware or Software   It is very important to determine if the problem originates in the software or in the hardware. For example, if a printer fails to print with one package, try it with another before concluding that the trouble is the printer. It could be that the software is faulty, or it might be a communications problem between the two. Testing components directly from the operating system is the most effective way because it is less likely to encounter communications problems.

Error Messages   Sometimes you may get an error message displayed on the screen or a control panel that can help you determine what the problem is. The key to such messages is usually found in the manual that accompanies the component. Record any such messages. They may be the key to the problem but sometimes the message does not recur and is then lost.

Reboot   If you get a persistent error message (especially from the computer itself) or another indicator of trouble, try a reboot or restart of the system by turning it off for a few seconds and then turning it back on and beginning all over. Occasionally your system may experience a **glitch,** which is a problem of unknown origin that does not recur. Also, computers sometimes "lock up," and you must reboot them to regain control. Please note that anytime you turn off an electronic component, always wait at least 15 seconds before turning it back on. Restoring the power immediately carries a small risk of causing a circuit failure.

On most systems you may reboot in either of two ways: the cold boot from the power-off condition, or the warm boot from the keyboard or a Reset button with the power on. A warm boot is usually sufficient to eliminate error conditions, glitches, and locked systems, but in some cases the problem is not resolved until a cold boot is performed.

Diagnostics and Test Patterns   You can often generate a helpful error message by the use of diagnostic routines or test patterns. If the problem appears to involve part of the computer or disk units and your computer comes with diagnostic routines, run these and see if you get an error code. If a component such as a printer or modem seems to be malfunctioning, look for an error code or light on its control panel. Many of these products have a self-test pattern that can sometimes be of help.

Boards   If you have installed any extra boards in your computer, double-check all of these to be sure they are firmly seated in the correct slots. Be certain that none of the prongs or pins along the edge of the boards is bent, broken, or missing. If you can find no other obvious problem, remove the boards that you inserted and try the system without them. If it works, replace each, *one at a time,* and recheck the performance until you find the trouble.

Communications   The computer and a peripheral must both be set to communicate at the same **baud rate** (see Chapter 4). For example, if a computer is set up at 9,600 baud for the printer port and 2,400 baud for the modem port, then the printer and modem must also be set to 9,600 and

2,400 baud, respectively. (The proper baud rate is usually determined by the peripheral and can be found in the corresponding manual.)

DIP Switches   Many components have DIP or other switches that must be properly set. DIP switches are usually found in sets of eight small switches in a row, each of which can be set to either On or Off. Sometimes several panels of DIP switches are present. Here is a simplified example of a typical DIP switch setting chart for a printer.

DIP Switch Selection Chart

Switch	Function if ON	Function if OFF
1	Serial mode	Parallel mode
2	IBM emulation	Epson emulation
3	Standard ASCII set	Extended ASCII set
4	8½″ page default	8″ page default
5	Automatic line-feed advance with each carriage return	No automatic line-feed
6	Skip ½″ space at perforations	No skip
7	Paper out signal	No paper out signal
8	Print DEL character	Ignore DEL character

If you wish to use a parallel connection with IBM emulation and the standard ASCII character set, you would set the first three switches to Off, On, and On, respectively. If you are uncertain about or don't understand some of the switch settings, leave them at the factory preset default positions since these are preferred by most users.

DIP switches are commonly used to select various features, such as automatic modes, alternate character sets, emulation modes, baud rates, and other communications protocols. Sometimes two or more switches are used to set a feature. These switches are normally located either at the rear of the unit, on or under a control panel, or under some other cover. The key to the various switch combinations is found in the operating manual for that component.

Troubleshooting Software Problems

If your system hardware checks out and it functions properly with some of your software packages but not with others, then the problem may well be with the software. This does not mean that it is necessarily defective; there are a number of possible problems and solutions.

Error Messages   Note and record any error messages. These are usually listed and explained in the accompanying documentation. The presence of an error message is often an indication of a problem but not a defect, and it can be the clue to the source of the trouble and its solution.

Reload   If a program does not load properly, try reloading it. Some computers or programs (or a particular combination) tend to be temperamental at times and may occasionally require more than one attempt to load. (Cassette-based systems are especially sensitive to this problem.) Reloading is a possible remedy anytime you experience a software failure.

System and Version   If your computer runs more than one operating system or more than one release of the same operating system, be sure that each application software package is compatible with the operating system or version that you are currently using. (This is not a consideration for many computers and programs.)

If a program loads but does not appear to function properly, it is probably a communication problem, either between you and the software or between the software and part of the system. Software packages should run properly the first time on your computer. If you are having a consistent problem with most or all of your programs, then you may have a more serious difficulty. Either you are not performing the installations and operations of the programs correctly, or there is a compatibility problem somewhere within the system.

Commands   Verify that commands are being entered correctly. For example, some programs require that all commands be entered using only uppercase letters. Also, do not confuse similar characters such as *0* (zero) and O (oh) and *1* (one) and *l* (ell), which may be interchangeable on a typewriter but not on a computer keyboard.

Responses   Be certain that your responses to program inquiries are proper. If you do not give a proper response to a question, some programs may not know what to do, usually resulting in unexpected (and probably unwelcome) results.

Protocols There could be a difference in the way a program tries to address a part of your system, such as the printer or the monitor screen, and the way that device expects to be addressed. For example, the codes that a program sends to a printer to initiate different print fonts, pitches, and enhancements may not be the same as those that the printer requires. If this is the case and your software package does not have a configuration program (see following) that will solve the problem, ask your dealer about having the software **patched** or modified so that it will use the proper codes.

It also could be that you do not have all the hardware required by the software. For example, if a program makes use of graphics and your computer does not have that capability, then you cannot make use of that feature. The hardware and software must be compatible. If you have an EGA board, then the software must honor that graphics system. This cannot be patched.

Configuration Many of the professional-level packages come with a configuration or installation program that permits you to customize the specific package to your individual hardware. They allow you to specify things such as the type of terminal or printer you are using, communications protocols for modems, screen highlights (such as type and color), and specific codes for printer protocols. Unfortunately, even the best of these programs cannot anticipate and handle all users' needs; thus you may find that an installed version of a program still has some communications difficulties and may need to be patched.

Write-Protection One final possibility is one that is more likely to occur after you have used your system for a while. This involves trying to write data to a disk or file that has been write-protected. If the problem seems to occur only when you attempt to save a file, check to see if the diskette has a write-protection tab in place or is otherwise guarded. Also, examine the file directory (see the next section) to see if it lists the file that you are working with as "R/O" (or some other designation for read-only) or another protected status.

Getting Acquainted

You may also need to become familiar with many of the operating system commands and **system utility** files. These are used for such jobs as formatting and copying disks; creating, changing, and playing directories; deleting, renaming, printing, and copying files; making backups; and checking the system status. All of these processes are the same in principle for all systems, but the commands required to achieve them vary widely. Also, some models do not require some of these operations, such as creating or changing directories and checking the system status. Here is a brief description of some operations.

Formatting Disks must be prepared to receive data. This process initializes a disk and sets it up to record data in the format used by the system. Any data already on a disk is erased when it is formatted. Formatting is usually done by a system utility program and a simple command.

Backups You need to make a backup copy of all your software where it is permitted. Not all software can or should be copied, and sometimes only selected parts of a package are available for copy. Check your license agreement for the rules on this. Normally, the original disk is then *write-protected and placed in a safe place* and the new copy becomes the working copy.

If you have a floppy disk system, then you simply copy the files onto a second diskette. This can usually be done either by individual files, using a formatted disk and a file copy program, or for the entire disk, using a disk copy program. For a hard disk the separate files are copied onto that unit and then appropriate backups made.

Directories If you have a disk-based system, you can generate a list or directory of the files on the disk or a particular section of the disk. The information displayed with a directory varies with the system, but a typical directory listing might look something like this:

```
Directory of Disk A:
   Name    Type Size Access  Created   Changed
  DATAPLUS LTR    4k   R/W   2-29-88   2-29-88
  MAIN     DCT  158k   R/O  10-22-87  10-22-87
  RESUME   DOC    7k   R/W   2-15-88   2-28-88
  SOFTPRO  LTR    4k   R/W   3-04-88   3-05-88
  SPELL    COM   27k   R/O  10-22-87  10-22-87
  SUPP1    DCT    2k   R/W  11-09-87   6-30-88
  UNITECH  LTR    4k   R/W   2-29-88   2-29-88
  WORDPRO  COM   62k   R/O  10-22-87  10-22-87
Space Remaining: 92k
```

Most of this display should be self-explanatory, but a complete description of the directories available for your system can be found in the system software documentation.

Once you are satisfied that everything (including all software) is in working order, you are ready to become acquainted with your new computer and learn all about what it can do. Take your time. A single software package can take days or even weeks to master, and there may be features you never need. Work with a program until you understand and feel comfortable with it. Don't try to memorize all the commands; they will become familiar with use.

Read Your Documentation   When you select a program to run, first scan the accompanying documentation. This usually tells you how to begin and provides a brief description of the available features and commands. There may also be sample sessions, a tutorial section (or separate manual), or a demonstration disk to help you learn about and use the program. You can then study the manual in detail as you master each feature and capability.

Try It Out   Don't be reluctant to try things. *The only way you will learn is to do.* You cannot physically harm your computer's hardware with any command from the keyboard. Also, if you exercise reasonable care and common sense, the chances are remote that you will accidentally damage or destroy any software or data files that you have created. *Think before you use the keyboard.* If you do not know what a particular command will do, then don't use it—unless you have some assurance that whatever it does will be harmless. Should you accidentally lose a program or data file, you should be able to restore it from your backup copy. If it is a protected program that you cannot copy, most companies will replace damaged disks at a minimal charge.

Ask for Help   If all your attempts to solve a problem or master a particular program fail, ask for help before you give up in frustration and disappointment. A good place to start is a local full-service dealer, another user, or a computer professional who has experience with your model computer and the particular item that is giving you trouble. Also, most major software companies provide telephone support for their products, but many of these are available only to licensed owners and only during normal business hours, when it may not be convenient to you.

Report Problems   Sometimes a problem is not discovered until you have used a product for a while. If you cannot resolve the difficulty, consult your dealer or the manufacturer. They should be able to give you possible solutions and, in the case of some software, perhaps even provide a free corrected version.

Misrepresentations

If you did an adequate job with your pre-purchase homework and were careful in selecting your system and dealer, you should have no unpleasant surprises. However, if you find that a product has been misrepresented or does not perform according to its reported standards, don't delay: Discuss your concerns with the retailer from whom you purchased the item. It's possible that you are not using it properly or have misinterpreted something. If there is a gap between performance and claims, however, you do not have to just accept an inferior product. Certain remedies are available to you.

First, ask your dealer to make an appropriate adjustment. If this fails to resolve the problem to your satisfaction, there are several things you can do or sources you can contact for possible assistance. A letter or phone call to the manufacturer is often of help. The local Better Business Bureau or Chamber of Commerce may also be of value. The Better Business Bureau offers a mediation or arbitration service and is frequently very useful in resolving such disputes. Your local or state Department of Consumer Affairs can provide you with information on local laws and your rights regarding such things as cash refunds, merchandise exchanges, implied warranties, fair advertising practices, and so forth. (This is information that may be of value to you *before* you make your purchase.) If you have a local television or radio station or a newspaper with an active consumer reporter, this can be an especially powerful lever because of the potentially adverse publicity for the store.

A company is sometimes less cooperative when they have all your money from the sale. If you paid for your purchase by credit card, you may be able to stop or delay part or all of the payment from the bank. There is usually a time limit on this sort of action, however, and if you do not prevail, it could cost you extra interest charges. If the problem involves a mail-order sale, you have very specific rights with this sort of purchase. Consult the U.S. Post Office (or other shipper) for information as soon as possible. Finally, if the problem involves a substantial amount of money and you feel you have really been wronged, you might consult an attorney for advice and possible legal action. Sometimes a letter with the proper letterhead and wording will do the trick.

The two best ways to protect and ensure your rights after a sale are to do your homework in advance and above all, keep careful written records of all transactions. If a dispute should arise, you will have a much better chance of prevailing when your position is well documented and supported in writing.

Preparing for Work

A system that is handled and maintained in a sloppy manner is a disaster waiting to happen. You may experience a serious problem such as the loss of data or equipment damage that could have been prevented by a few pre-planned precautions. Here are a few suggestions that might help you avoid such difficulties.

Establish Good Work Habits It is a very good idea to establish basic guidelines for the use of your system. These should be for everyone who uses it. Everyone should be familiar with the basic start-up and shut-down procedures as well as any software packages that will be used. Each user should work to maintain the basic organization of the overall system. If several people regularly use the disks, it is normally better for one person to take charge of disk "housekeeping" chores and the making of backups. This is safer and has less potential for a misunderstanding that might cause a backup or other job to be left undone. This might also be the person to troubleshoot any problems that may arise. All items associated with the use of the computer should be kept in a specific place when not in use. Routine maintenance such as changing paper and ribbons in the printer should be shared by all except very young children.

The environment you provide for your computer equipment can make the difference between years or only months between breakdowns. Establish set rules relating to food, beverages, smoking, pets, chewing gum, open windows, use of sprays, and other potential hazards to your system. Be sure that each user understands the damage that is possible from such hazards. Simple chores, such as the replacement of dust covers and putting diskettes away properly, can make a difference in time, especially if your system must exist in a dusty environment. Finally, routine dusting and other external cleaning duties should be shared by all as the need arises.

Get Organized Arrange your materials in an orderly fashion. Keep all of your documentation and other written materials, including printed copies of files, neatly organized and ready for quick reference. No matter how many times you use a particular software package, you may still find the need to consult the manual at times. Your active diskettes should be kept with up-to-date labels and stored to provide quick access to their files. In like manner, all diskettes or tapes used as backup should be carefully labeled and arranged by some convenient system.

If you have a disk system, as most computers do, you should keep the contents of any disk free of unwanted or unnecessary files. Whenever a file is no longer of value, delete it from the disk. You can always save a copy of it on a backup diskette until you no longer need it. A hard disk system may permit the creation of multiple directories for different uses. Take advantage of this feature and organize your disk according to its major uses. For example, this might mean one directory for games, one for word processing files, one for spreadsheet work, and so forth. You can always change or delete the directories as necessary, files can be moved from one to another, and a program in one directory can use a data file in another.

Plan a Backup System   It is important to maintain a current backup copy of all your software (where it is permitted) and the files that you create. Without this, you may not be able to recover lost data. The backup system and procedures you use are to a great extent a matter of personal choice, but there are a few general suggestions that you might find useful.

You need to keep a permanent backup copy of your operating system and application software, but there is generally no need to recopy these files every time you do a backup unless they have changed. Most backups need only involve the files that have been created or changed since the last backup. This can be done manually, but the selection of the files that have been created or changed since the last backup can be tedious and time consuming. There are software packages for performing backups that will automatically back up only those files that are new or have been modified since the last backup.

If you have a hard disk, you might use a tape system for major backups of the entire disk, and diskettes for backing up selected files. If certain files are very important or sensitive, or would be extremely difficult or impossible to replace, you might make two backups and keep one in a physically separate location. Thus, if the room where the computer is kept is damaged, perhaps by fire or a storm, you would still have a copy intact.

Never make a backup copy on the tape or diskette that contains the most recent prior backup. If there was a failure during the copy procedure (rare but not unknown), both the original and the backup copy could be lost. Use some type of alternating system that makes use of two or preferably three tapes or diskettes that are used in rotation. (Using three copies in this way is known as the **grandfather system.**) Carefully label each as it is made with the date and contents.

How often you make a backup will depend on how often you use your computer, how much data you generate, and how sensitive and irreplaceable your data is. There is no rule that will apply to all users about when to make a backup, and each person has to establish a schedule for their own system, but the following rule of thumb is a good guideline: If the system is used constantly (all day), daily or alternate-day backups are probably needed. If the computer is used often (daily or nearly daily) but not constantly every day, then weekly or biweekly backups are probably sufficient. If the computer is used only occasionally, then monthly or bimonthly backups are likely all that will be needed. Clearly, if you generate important files, then you will need to perform frequent backups. But, even if the computer is used constantly but only for something such as playing games, which produce no new files, then there will be little need for backups.

Formatting Disks It is strongly recommended that you keep some or all of your extra floppy disks formatted in advance. (You should always have some spare diskettes on hand.) You may need a diskette to save a file and will not be able to stop and format one without losing your work. This situation can occur if you try to save a file on a disk that does not have enough space left to hold it; this is not an uncommon occurrence with floppy disk systems and could also happen with a hard disk as well. Many users routinely format all diskettes as soon as they get them.

Naming Files can be very important to the proper organization of your work. A file should be given a name that gives an indication of its purpose or use. Compare the following two directory listings for the same five files:

```
Directory of Disk A:
    Name    Type Size Access   Created   Changed
     C             9k    R/W    1-23-88   1-24-88
     C2           12k    R/W    3-13-88   3-13-88
     CM           18k    R/W   10-31-87   4-24-88
     VM            3k    R/W    1-25-88   1-25-88
     X            34k    R/W   11-04-88  12-07-88
Space Remaining: 284k
```

```
Directory of Disk A:
    Name    Type Size Access   Created   Changed
  CATHY1    LTR    9k    R/W    1-23-88   1-24-88
  CATHY2    LTR   12k    R/W    3-13-88   3-13-88
  CLUBMINS  RPT   18k    R/W   10-31-87   4-24-88
  VALUMART  LTR    3k    R/W    1-25-88   1-25-88
  XMAS      LST   34k    R/W   11-04-88  12-07-88
Space Remaining: 284k
```

Judge for yourself. If you were not sure exactly what was on this disk, which listing would be more helpful?

With a few possible restrictions, you can usually name a file anything you want. You may be limited to a certain number of characters (eight was assumed above), and some symbols might not be permitted (such as an asterisk, question mark, colon, and period) because they have a special meaning. Some files require that you specify it as a certain type, such as BAS for a program written in BASIC, WP for a word processing file, DBD for data to be processed by a data base manager, and COM or EXE for command or executable files. Sometimes these are supplied by the system or software. Many times, however, you can select the type as well as the name, in which case you should try to make it meaningful by using something like DAT, LST, LTR, or RPT for a data file, a list, a letter, or a report, respectively. (The three-letter file type is technically known as the file **extension.**)

The simpler or more user-friendly the system, the less you will need to specify or name a file. Sometimes you have to do no more than supply the basic name, and all other needed items such as an extension are handled automatically. However, with other systems or software packages you have to supply additional parameters for a complete file **specification.** With a disk system you may have to add a device indicator to tell which drive or part of a drive you are using, and hard disks may even require a directory or account designation.

Caring for Your System

The key to taking care of your investment is to know and understand your system's vulnerable points. Generally, both computer hardware and software are very sturdy and will not fail because of any environmental problem. However, sometimes a minor matter can cause a major headache.

Hardware   Your manuals will give you recommendations for such things as the temperatures, humidity range, and maximum altitude for the optimum performance of each product. If you are perspiring, your computer may be getting too warm inside. This can shorten the life of delicate electronic components. Good ventilation is essential at all times for adequate air circulation and proper cooling of circuits. If the humidity is high enough to form moisture on surfaces, then this moisture is probably inside your system as well. If you are aware of pollution in the air or on surfaces, your system may even be far more sensitive to this than you are. A dust cover is both useful and recommended, especially for systems in rooms with open windows, but it should not be considered a panacea.

The read/write heads on a disk drive may ride as close as a few millionths of an inch above the disk surface and scan it at speeds in excess of 100 miles per hour. The gap between the head and disk surface is many times smaller than such tiny particles as those found in smoke or the thickness of a fingerprint. Larger, visible dust particles would be enormous to such a system. For this reason most high-speed, high-capacity disk drives are now fixed in a sealed unit, the most popular of which uses the **Winchester** technology. However, a few hard disks and all floppy disks are not sealed and are thus open to contamination from the environment.

While it is true that nonsealed disk units do not have such a small **head gap** or high speed, they are still sensitive to foreign substances. A dust particle can be ground between the disk and head, causing permanent damage to both. Less visible obstructions, such as fingerprints and very tiny particles from smoke or sprays, can be even more damaging as they build up over time. There is always the possibility that a large particle will be knocked out of the way; however, the smaller ones tend to be more tightly stuck to the surface and are more likely to be ground or smeared under the head and on the surface of the disk.

You should be aware that cigarette smoke is one of the greatest hazards your system faces. Smoke particles are very small and can get into places in quantity where larger ones cannot. This has the potential to damage not only the disk drives as described above but many other parts of the system as well. One very sensitive item is often the keyboard. Sometimes very tiny particles get under the key caps and, in time, interfere with the contact, causing a key to skip or repeat erratically.

One reason smoking around a computer is a significant risk to the system is that the smoker tends to blow the smoke forward and directly at the system. Any smoke can be harmful to your equipment, but if you smoke while using your computer, it would be better to direct the smoke away from the system. It would be even better if you arranged to take a break when you needed or wanted a smoke, and enjoy it in another room.

Sprays pose additional hazards. Some aerosols, such as cleaners, polishes, room fresheners, and personal grooming products, can cause a thin film to form on surfaces. The gummy buildup of these substances can be as damaging in time as the grinding from solid particles. *Never spray anything directly on your hardware that is not designed for that specific use, and never under any circumstances expose disk or tape surfaces to any sprays.* It would be best to avoid, if possible, spraying around unprotected equipment. If this is not practical, then take precautions to minimize the system's exposure to such potential hazards.

Finally, there is the potential hazard from electrical disturbances. These normally come from two sources: static electrical discharges and power surges or noise. We have all experienced a shock when we touch something in cold weather. This can be disastrous to a computer. Such sudden charges can destroy chips and the data on disks. You can buy nondamaging sprays or other products that will help eliminate this problem. Also available to reduce the problem are antistatic mats that can be placed under your computer or on the floor under your chair and feet.

Power surges and noise from the AC power line, which can be equally deadly to equipment and data, often occur without any indication. Devices that are available at a reasonable cost can provide protection from such interference except in extreme cases, as in a nearby lightning strike. It is strongly recommended that every system be protected by such a device. Your entire system should be isolated; unprotected components can send a surge back through a connecting cable, thus damaging elements you thought were protected. If you have a modem, don't forget that the telephone line should also be isolated.

Software can be damaged when a disk is physically scratched, or the data can be affected without any actual physical damage to the medium on which it is recorded. Practically anything that can harm your hardware—heat, humidity, dust, smoke, sprays—can also be a hazard to your software. Never leave diskettes in a closed car on a hot summer day. Dust and other airborne substances are probably the most common sources of physical damage to diskettes and tapes. Never leave software out of its protective jacket or container, and always store your software, preferably with diskettes upright, in a closed area. A contaminated diskette or tape is the most frequent cause of similar damage to a drive head.

Never place anything on top of a diskette because this can damage the recording surface. Tiny particles that have accumulated may grind and mar the delicate magnetic material. A diskette can become crimped or bent if left lying around on a table. Finally, when you label a diskette, never use a sharp pen or pencil or press down hard; use only a soft-tip pen or marker that requires little pressure to write.

The pattern of magnetic images on a disk or tape can also be damaged, with a resulting loss of the associated information without any actual physical harm to the surface. This can occur from adverse environmental conditions such as heat and humidity. If these conditions are severe enough to disturb the data, however, they will usually harm the surface as well. There is one notable and very important exception: magnetic fields. Static sparks are an example of this effect. A disk or tape exposed to a magnetic field can have part or all of its data erased, and you may not even be aware of it until you try to use it.

Magnetic fields are fairly common in the home. Any electrical device generates one to some extent, but, fortunately, magnetic fields are generally fairly weak and not strong enough to cause a problem except around certain appliances or other electrical units. There are two considerations: how large the current is and how close to it one gets. Televisions or monitors, transformers, large speaker magnets (in stereos), vacuum cleaners, compressors, and some power tools generate substantial magnetic fields. Software has been lost simply by placing it on top of a monitor. Even the transformers in stereo amplifiers or other power supplies have been known to cause similar damage. Never place any magnetic media on or near an electrical device that is not designed for it. Don't forget about permanent magnets such as those that decorate the refrigerator.

Supplies   Treat your extra supplies with the same care that you do the ones currently in use. Store items in a cool, dry, and clean place until needed.

Cleaning Your System   Computers require relatively little physical maintenance. For most systems a good screen cleaner and a small vacuum or soft brush is all that is needed to maintain the external surfaces.

A few simple cautions should be observed when cleaning your system's external surfaces:

- Never clean your computer with any part of the system turned on. To help avoid generating static charges always turn off the entire system at least five minutes before cleaning any surfaces.
- Never use a wet cloth. Use only a dry or slightly damp cloth, or an approved cleaner in spray form.
- Never use strong soaps or detergents, furniture polishes, window cleaners, and so forth; such substances can cause irreparable damage to a system.
- Never use strong commercial cleaners, such as alcohol, acetone, and ammonia.
- Never spray anything on a dusty surface such as a keyboard. The tiny particles can cake and form a sticky layer in hard-to-reach areas that will be both damaging and difficult to remove.
- Never use a strong vacuum cleaner on delicate mechanical parts such as keyboards and printers.

The best way to "clean" your system is to do whatever you can to prevent it from needing to be cleaned. But when it does, *use only cleaners designed for use on computer component surfaces*. If for some reason you must clean a part of your system and a special cleaner is not available, you can use a cloth *slightly* dampened with either clear water or a *very mild* soapy solution.

Inventory Your System   Maintain an up-to-date record of your system. This should be an itemized list that reflects all components (including software), specific models (versions or releases for software, if available), all serial numbers where available, the value, and the date and place acquired. You may wish to keep this on your system, using a data base manager or other program, but you should always keep a printed copy of the current system components in a safe place. This could prove to be of real value for insurance or other purposes in case of theft, damage, or destruction of part or all of the system.

If you make a practice of specially marking your possessions, you should take care when doing so with delicate electronic equipment. Avoid the direct use of an electric engraving tool on any component that contains boards; such devices can damage the fragile chips on these boards. If you wish to use an electric engraving tool, physically separate the part on which you will be engraving from the delicate internal circuits before you begin. Preferable alternatives include mechanical engravers and stick-on labels.

Insurance   Do not assume that your homeowner's or other insurance coverage routinely covers your computer system. Some policies do not include computer equipment. Check with your agent to verify your company's policy. If your system is not covered, it can usually be protected at a small cost by the addition of a rider to your current policy.

Choosing Supplies

Most items, such as paper, diskettes, tapes, and printer ribbons, can be acquired for a discount if you purchase them in quantity. With the possible exception of ribbons, which will dry out if exposed to the air for an extended period of time, most items will keep indefinitely when properly stored.

Look for quality products. If you see a dealer selling something such as disks or paper at an unbelievably low price, beware and check it out carefully. Be sure to verify the specifications to ensure that you are getting what you want and need. Also, ask about the quality of the product. All DS/DD (double-sided/double-density) floppy disks or 20-pound (20#) paper stocks are not created equally. Often items that carry a certain rating or specification only minimally meet that standard and may be disappointing to you, either aesthetically or in their performance. If tempted but still in doubt, order a limited test supply.

Many of the larger independent companies now offer their own in-house brands of such things as ribbons, diskettes, and tapes. These are usually somewhat cheaper than the most popular, nationally known name brands, but you should be cautious. You may find that the nominal extra cost for a familiar brand is well justified.

Floppy Disks   You will find the specifications for the floppy disks your system uses in your manual. As mentioned in Chapter 4, floppy disks come in three sizes—8, 5¼, and 3½ inches—but the 8-inch type is almost never used on microcomputers anymore. There are three basic considerations when buying floppy disks: single- or double-sided, the **density,** and the **sectoring.** Your drive will use either one or both sides of the diskette. You can use double-sided disks in a single-sided drive but not vice versa. To record data on both sides of a disk with a single-sided drive, you have to take out the disk and turn it over. This may not work with all drives. A second write-protection notch (see following) may have to be cut.

Density refers to how much data can be recorded on the disk and is usually referred to as **single, double, quad,** or **high.** It may also be given in tracks per inch **(tpi),** as 48 or 96 tpi. You can always use a higher density than required, but never go to a lower one. It may work, but you run a significantly higher risk of errors and data loss.

Sectoring refers to how the beginning of the **sectors,** or parts of the data **tracks,** are marked by the system. Most systems now use a **soft-sectoring** method in which a single small hole near the center of the diskette is used to begin sectoring on each track. A few systems may still use **hard-sectoring** in which a series of holes (usually 10 or 16) mark the beginning of each sector. These two types of disks are not interchangeable.

Nearly all floppy disks have a **write-protection** method. This provides you with a means to protect the data on the disk from being accidentally erased or overwritten. On a 5½-inch diskette, a write-protection tab is placed over a small notch on the side of the disk. The system works in reverse on the older 8-inch floppy disks, and a small switch is used on the newest 3½-inch diskettes.

You would be wise to buy diskettes of good to high quality; these can now be found for under $1 or $2 each, depending on the type. The better the quality of the disk, the less likely you are to have a data loss because of a disk failure. You can use less expensive disks safely for the storage of backup or archival data, which are not used very frequently. Be wary of any diskette (except 3½-inch) that does not have a hub ring to reinforce the center hole. Such disks can be easily mangled by the drive mechanism. Hub rings can be bought separately and added.

Tapes   If you have a tape system that uses regular audio or video cassettes, you may find that it will not function properly with economy tapes. It is wise to buy the higher quality tapes or even the special **data cassettes** designed specifically for this purpose. Tape prices vary widely with the type and size, but you should expect to pay at least $5 to $10 for quality cassettes.

Paper   Printer paper is available in virtually any size, weight, quantity, quality, and design that you could want. Most people use either single sheets or the continuous **fan-fold** type that is divided by pages, but roll paper can still be found if that best suits your needs. Most stores that sell computer supplies have the more popular types. Many other varieties, ranging from unique sizes to paper preprinted with a letterhead or form blank, can be special-ordered.

The two most popular sizes are 14⅞ × 11 inches for wide carriage work and 9½ × 11 inches for standard carriages. Many of the latter type are perforated along each side to tear down to a standard size of 8½ × 11 inches. Several other sizes are commonly available as well, and multipart (carboned) forms can be found up to four parts. You can even get paper that has been prepunched for a 3-ring binder. In many cases you will have your choice between solid white (or another color), the traditional one-half-inch green bar, or some other pattern.

Paper comes in a variety of weights, ranging from about 12 to 20 pounds. A 15-pound stock is less expensive, for example, than the 20-pound and works in most printers. However, many users prefer the added strength and reliability of the heavier forms. It is less likely to jam. When comparing the price of different papers, look at the number of forms per carton. Because the pages get thicker the heavier the stock, there are fewer pages with increased weight. However, heavier does not always mean higher quality. Look for key words—*bond, fiber,* or *watermark*—if that is what you want.

If you do much printing, you may want to keep more than one type of paper on hand. Aside from the obvious advantages of having more than one size, there can be an economic advantage to using a cheaper and/or lighter stock for printing rough drafts and development work, and a better stock for the printing of finished products. Some people use continuous forms for the former and single sheets of high-quality bond or fiber paper for the latter.

A regular box of fan-fold paper of about 2,500 to 3,500 single sheets costs from $25 to $50. The price varies with the size, weight, and quality. A box of 20-pound paper may *appear* to cost less than a similar 15-pound stock, but it contains fewer sheets, so the net price is probably higher. Multiple-part forms and odd sizes are more expensive, as are the smaller boxes that are frequently offered. With the smaller boxes of 500 to 1,500 sheets, you normally pay much more for the same amount of paper than if you bought it in larger cartons. You are paying for the convenience of the smaller size, which is much easier to carry and move about. Smaller cartons weigh only a few pounds, whereas large boxes can exceed 50 pounds.

It may take a little experimenting to find the right paper for you and your printer. Remember when you are selecting fan-fold-type paper for a particular application, you will have to take the extra time to separate the sheets and that you may have some waste from tears or uneven separations. Not all fan-fold papers separate easily or smoothly, sometimes tearing or leaving ragged edges. Such paper is also more likely to jam because of the use of sprocket holes for feeding through the printer. Also, paper with the side perforations may not tear evenly either. Paper advertised as having "fine-perforations" may not be any better or even worse. You may have to try several brands of paper before you find one that is suitable to you.

Ribbons   Ribbons are relatively easy to purchase, since you generally buy the one for your particular model printer. However, the amount of inking can vary widely from one brand to another and is not necessarily reflected in the price. You might shop around and try different ribbons until you find one that suits you best. You may also find a significant price variation between ribbons from different companies.

Storage   Inexpensive yet very serviceable storage devices are available for your floppy disks, tapes, and other sensitive materials. These range from small units that store only about ten diskettes to large files that have the capacity to handle hundreds. You will likely find these storage devices very helpful and well worth the usually modest price. There are frugal alternatives. For example, you can make a floppy disk storage file from a sturdy shoe box and a little cardboard and tape, or you can store tapes in a box that contained a small appliance (such as a toaster). Some people even use the original packaging to store disks and tapes.

Cleaners   Obtain only recommended cleaning materials for your computer. Nondamaging cleaners (which are often also antistatic) are available from most computer stores for a few dollars and are excellent for cleaning monitor screens and other external surfaces. Small microvacuum cleaners are excellent for removing tiny dust particles from keyboards, printer mechanisms, and other hard-to-reach places. Cans of compressed air and a small brush can also be effective if used frequently.

Beware of cleaners for delicate parts of your system such as disk and tape unit heads. Many effective methods are available for this, but be careful about those that are abrasive or employ messy fluids. Use only nonabrasive, dry (or semidry) methods that clean with minimal intrusion into the physical mechanism of the drive. No cleaning system should be overused. You will have to judge how often to use a cleaner depending on how heavily the unit is used, but no more than once a month should be sufficient for most systems. Overuse can be harmful with some types of cleaning methods.

Miscellaneous Items   Virtually anything that you can think of or may need to assist you in your work and the enjoyment of your system has already been thought of and is for sale somewhere. You can get extra disk or tape labels, replacement write-protection tabs, and jackets for diskettes. Printout binders are available in any size, color, quality, and style that you can imagine. There are storage and filing systems for virtually anything and in any size. If you have a printer that uses a printwheel, there are catalogs with hundreds of these in a tremendous array of fonts and pitches. Preview your needs and purchase only what is necessary.

Updates and Upgrades

An **update** refers to the improvement of a product through a newer or corrected version. You may have an opportunity to acquire updates for many of your software packages but are not likely to change a hardware component for a newer model unless it is totally unsatisfactory. Many software vendors will notify you periodically of updates to their programs that you have purchased and registered with them. There is no reason to discourage you from obtaining these new versions, but you should remember that any special installation or modification that was required with the older release will likely be necessary with the newer one as well.

Occasionally a new release can introduce certain compatibility problems that you did not have previously. For example, if you are still using an old version of the operating system and have not updated it, a new release might not function properly with the older operating system. Such problems are the exception to the rule; most updates work as well if not better than the preceding editions. It is also rare that a new release does not function properly without some additional hardware component that was not previously required, such as a math coprocessor.

An **upgrade** refers to the changing of part or all of a system to a more powerful version. This can be an expensive and complex proposition. In some respects you are starting all over with a new system. However, you probably already have a substantial investment in hardware, software, and your own data files that you need to preserve as much as possible. Also, the existence of these items can make it even harder to assemble an upgrade system that both suits your needs and preserves your files.

Some companies have a good record with respect to their **upgrade path,** or the ability to change to the hardware of a newer or more powerful model and still maintain compatibility with older peripherals and software, while others do not. If you purchase a system without regard to potential upgrades because you feel that you will have no need for them but later find that you do, don't despair.

The upgrade path usually involves changing the basic computer to a later version. This may, in turn, cause compatibility problems with parts from the older system—most frequently but not always the software. Some of your software programs may not be transferable, but your data files may be by simply moving them to a new disk with the new system format. You may also be able to gain new copies of much of your software without having to pay the full purchase price again. Ask your dealer to help you with this or write the software companies and explain the problem; some may exchange disks with you for a small fee. Moving to an upgrade can also introduce problems of compatibility with the older system peripherals, but this problem is not as common as the one encountered with the software. Fortunately, few personal computer owners are ever faced with the need to do a true upgrade.

Appendix A

Manufacturers Resource Guide

The following is a list of many of the most popular manufacturers of computers and components, along with contact information. The presence of a company on the list is not to be interpreted as a recommendation or endorsement, nor is the absence of a manufacturer to be considered a disqualification. This list is not intended to be comprehensive but is offered here only as a convenience in helping you to contact companies in order to gather information on their products. (Companies that provide only services or supplies have not been included.)

Acer Technologies Corp., 401 Charcot Ave., San Jose, CA 95131, 408-922-0333

Adobe Systems, Inc., 1585 Charleston Rd., P.O. Box 7900, Mountain View, CA 94039-7900, 800-344-8335, 415-961-4400

Adtek, 3706 Realty Rd., Dallas, TX 75244, 214-241-5811

Advanced Graphics Software, 333 W. Maude Ave., Suite 105, Sunnyvale, CA 94086, 408-749-8620

Advanced Logic Research, 10 Chrysler, Irvine, CA 92718, 714-581-6770

Advanced Professional Technologies, Inc., 715 Galveston, Redwood City, CA 94063, 415-366-4600

AEG Olympia, Box 22, Somerville, NJ 08876-0022, 800-999-6872

AlphaNumeric, Inc., 14060 Gannet St., Suite 1-103, Santa Fe Springs, CA 90670, 213-921-8689

Alpha Software Corp., One North Ave., Burlington, MA 01803, 800-451-1018 (800-462-2016 in MA), 617-229-2924

Alps America, 3553 North First St., San Jose, CA 95134, 800-825-ALPS (800-257-7872 in CA)

Alps Electric, Inc., 3553 North First St., San Jose, CA 95134, 408-432-6000

ALR see **Advanced Logic Research**

Amax Engineering Corp., 47315 Mission Falls Ct., Fremont, CA 94539, 800-888-AMAX, 415-651-8886

Amdek Corp., 2201 Lively Blvd., Elk Grove Village, IL 60007, 312-364-1180

American Micro Technology, 14751-B Franklin Ave., Tustin, CA 92680, 714-731-6800, 213-477-6320

American Mitac Corp., 3385 Viso Ct., Santa Clara, CA 95054, 408-988-0258, 800-321-8344

American Power Conversion, 350 Columbia St., P.O. Box 3723, Peace Dale, RI 02883, 401-789-5735

American Small Business Computers, Inc., 327 S. Mill St., Prior, OK 74361, 918-826-4844

AMQ Computer Corp., 655 N. Pastoria Ave., Sunnyvale, CA 94086, 408-245-2310

Anderson Jacobson, 521 Charcot Ave., San Jose, CA 95131, 408-435-8520

AOC International USA, Ltd., 10991 NW Airworld Dr., Kansas City, MO 64153, 800-443-7516, 816-891-8066

Applause Software, P.O. Box 4104, Salt Lake City, UT 84110, 800-544-2049, 801-596-0091

Apple Computer, Inc., 20525 Mariani Ave., Cupertino, CA 95014, 408-996-1010, 408-973-2222

Aprotek, 1071-A Avenido Acaso, Camarillo, CA 93010, 800-962-5800

ARK Electronic Products, 325 W. Hibiscus Blvd., Melbourne, FL 32901, 305-724-5260

Ashton-Tate, 20101 Hamilton Ave., Torrance, CA 90502-1319, 800-437-4329 (303-799-4900 in CO)

AST Research, 2121 Alton Ave., Irvine, CA 92714, 714-553-0340; 16950 Armstrong, Irvine, CA 92714, 800-792-9270

AT&T Information Systems, One Speedwell Ave., Morristown, NJ 07960, 800-247-1212

Atari, Inc., 1312 Crossman, Sunnyvale, CA 94086, 408-745-4851

ATI Technologies, Inc., 3761 Victoria Park Ave., Scarborough, Ontario, Canada M1W 3S2, 416-756-0718

Austin Computer Systems, Inc., 10300 Metric Blvd., Austin, TX 78758, 512-458-5106

Autocontrol Inc., 11400 Dorsett Rd., St. Louis, MO 63043, 314-739-0055

Baby Micro, Inc., 7388 S. Revere Pkwy., Suite 708, Englewood, CO 80112, 303-790-7717

Basic Time, Inc., 3040 Oakmead Village Dr., Santa Clara, CA 95051, 408-727-0877

Basis International, 5901 Jefferson St. NE, Albuquerque, NM 87109, 800-423-1394, 505-345-5232

Bentley Computer Products, 1700 Still Meadows Cove, Round Rock, TX 78681, 800-626-4027, 512-250-9897

BLOC Publishing Corp., 800 SW 37th Ave., Suite 765, Coral Gables, FL 33134, 800-888-2562

Blue Chip Electronics, Inc., 7305 W. Boston St., Chandler, AZ 85226, 602-961-1485

Borland, 1159 Triton Dr., Foster City, CA 94404, 800-345-2888

Boss Technology, 6050 McDonough Dr., Norcross, GA 30093, 404-840-0886

Brightbill-Roberts & Co., Ltd., 120 E. Washington St., Suite 421, Syracuse, NY 13202, 800-444-3490, 315-474-3400

Brightwork Development Corp., P.O. Box 8728, Red Bank, NJ 07701, 800-552-9876, 201-530-0440

Broderbund Software, P.O. Box 12947, San Rafael, CA 94913-2947, 800-527-6263

Brother International Corp., 8 Corporate Place, Piscataway, NJ 08854, 201-981-0300

CAD Systems Unlimited, Inc., 5201 Great American Pkwy., #443, Santa Clara, CA 95054, 408-562-5762

Canon USA, Inc., One Canon Plaza, Lake Success, NY 11042, 516-488-6700

Caseworks, Inc., 1 Dunwoody Park, #130, Atlanta, GA 30338, 404-399-6236

Central Point Software, Inc., 9700 SW Capitol Hwy., Portland, OR 97219, 503-244-5782

Chi Corp., 26055 Emery Rd., Cleveland, OH 44128, 800-828-0311, 216-831-2622

Chinon America, Inc., 660 Maple Ave., Torrance, CA 60503, 800-441-0222 (213-533-0274 in CA)

CIE Systems, Inc., 2515 McCabe Way, P.O. Box 19628, Irvine, CA 92713, 800-437-2341, 714-660-1800

Cipher Data Products, Inc., 2101 Commonwealth Blvd., Ann Arbor, MI 48105, 800-424-7437

Citizen America Corp., 2401 Colorado Ave., Suite 190, Santa Monica, CA 90404, 213-453-0614

Club American Technologies, 341 W. Warren Ave., Fremont, CA 94539, 415-683-6600

CMS Enhancements, Inc., 1372 Valencia Ave., Tustin, CA 92680, 714-259-9555

Commodore Business Machines, Inc., 1200 Wilson Dr., West Chester, PA 19380, 215-431-9100

Compaq Computer Corp., 20333 FAA 149, Houston, TX 77070, 800-231-0900

Compukit see **Hard Drive Specialist**

Computer Associates International, Inc., 1240 McKay Dr., San Jose, CA 95131, 800-531-5236

Computer Peripherals, Inc., 2635 Lavery Ct., Suite 5, Newbury Park, CA 91320, 800-854-7600, 805-499-5751

Computer Products United, Inc., 12803 Schabarum Ave., Irwindale, CA 91706, 800-824-2936 (800-662-6111 in CA)

Concentric Data Systems, Inc., 18 Lyman St., Westboro, MA 01581, 800-325-9035 (508-366-1122 in MA)

Concept Omega Corp., 19 Schoolhouse Rd., P.O. Box 6712, Somerset, NJ 08875-9958, 201-560-1377

Control Systems, 2675 Patton Rd., P.O. Box 64750, St. Paul, MN 55164, 800-826-4281, 612-631-7800

Cordata, Inc., 2001 Corporate Center Dr., Newbury Park, CA 91320, 805-375-1500

COREL, 1600 Carling Ave., Ottawa, Ontario, Canada K1Z 8R7, 613-728-8200

CPT Corp., 8100 Mitchell Rd., P.O. Box 295, Eden Prairie, MN 55344, 612-937-8000

Crosstalk Communications, 1000 Holcomb Woods Pkwy., Roswell, GA 30076-2575, 404-998-3998

CTS Fabri-Tek, Inc., 6900 Shady Oak Rd., Eden Prairie, MN 55344, 800-328-6104 (612-941-9100 in MN)

CTX International, Inc., 20768 Carrey Rd., Walnut, CA 91789, 714-595-6146

Cypernetronics, Inc., 15 Deer Ct., Sacramento, CA 95823, 916-428-2100

DACEasy, Inc., 17950 Preston Rd., Suite 800, Dallas, TX 75252, 800-877-8088

DataEase International, 7 Cambridge Dr., Trumbull, CT 06611, 800-3344-EASE (203-374-8000 in CT)

Data Facility, Inc., 1691 W. Hamlin, Rochester Hills, MI 48063, 313-583-0550

Datafox Computer Products, 2215 E. University, Phoenix, AZ 85034, 800-821-6317, 215-879-7080

Data Storm Technologies, Inc., P.O. Box 1471, Columbia, MO 65205, 314-478-8461

Data Technology Corp., 2775 Northwestern Pkwy., Santa Clara, CA 95051, 408-986-9545

Dataway Communications, Inc., 2941 Alton Ave., Irvine, CA 92714, 800-367-6555 (714-553-1555 in CA)

DEC see **Digital Equipment Corp.**

Dell Computer Corp., 9505 Arboretum Blvd., Austin, TX 78759-7299, 800-426-5150

Delrina Technology, Inc., 4454 Genessee St., Buffalo, NY 14225, 800-268-6082, 716-835-0405

Delta Technology International, 1621 Westgate Rd., Eau Claire, WI 54703, 800-242-6368, 715-832-7575

DFI, 2544 Port St., West Sacramento, CA 95691, 916-373-1234

Digital Communications Association, 1000 Alderman Dr., Alpharetta, GA 30201, 404-442-4000

Digital Composition Systems, 1750 W. Northern Ave., Second Floor, Phoenix, AZ 85021, 602-870-7667

Digital Equipment Corp., 146 Main St., Maynard, MA 01754, 800-842-5273

Digital Products, Inc., 108 Water St., Watertown, MA 02172, 800-243-2333, 617-924-1680

Digital Research, Inc., P.O. Box DRI, Monterey, CA 93942, 416-360-5316

Diversified Technology, 112 E. State St., Ridgeland, MS 39158, 800-443-2667, 601-856-4121

D-Link Systems, Inc., 3303 Harbor Blvd., Suite E-8, Costa Mesa, CA 92626, 714-549-7942

Dyna Computers, 3081 N. First St., San Jose, CA 95134, 408-943-0100

Dynamic Graphics, Inc., 6000 N. Forest Park Dr., Peoria, IL 61614, 800-255-8800

Dynamic Microprocessor Associates, Inc., 60 E. 42nd St., Suite 1100, New York, NY 10165, 212-687-7115

Dynatech Computer Power, Inc., 5800 Buffer Lane, Scotts Valley, CA 95066, 800-638-9098, 408-438-5760

E + E DataComm, 2115 Ringwood Ave., San Jose, CA 95131-1725, 408-288-8880

Electrochrome (U.S.A.), Ltd., 809 Wellington St. N., Kitchener, Ontario, Canada N2G 4J6, 519-744-7111

Emulex Corp., 3545 Harbor Blvd., Costa Mesa, CA 92626, 714-662-5600

Enabling Technologies, Inc., 600 S. Dearborn, #1304, Chicago, IL 60605, 800-544-0629, 312-427-0408

Epson America, Inc., 2780 Lomita Blvd., Torrance, CA 90505, 800-922-8911, 213-539-9140

Everex Systems, Inc., 48431 Milmont Dr., Fremont, CA 94538, 800-334-4552, 415-498-1111

EVI/Fastcomm Data Corp., 12347-E Sunrise Valley Dr., Reston, VA 22091, 800-521-2496

EZ-Logic, 315 S. El Monte, Los Altos, CA 94022, 800-635-6442 (800-544-4353 in CA), 415-949-2834

Fifth Generation Systems, Inc., 11200 Industriplex Blvd., Baton Rouge, LA 70809, 800-873-4384, 504-291-7221

Five Star Computers, 2100 N. Greenville Ave., Suite 200, Richardson, TX 75082, 800-752-5555

Fontex Technology, Inc., 600 S. Date Ave., Alhambra, CA 91803, 800-289-8299, 818-289-8299

Foresight Resources Corp., 10725 Ambassador Dr., Kansas City, MO 64153, 800-231-8574

Formworx Corp., Reservoir Place, 1601 Trapelo Rd., Waltham, MA 02154, 800-992-0085, 617-890-4499

Fox Software, 118 W. South Boundary, Perrysburg, OH 43551, 419-874-0162

Franklin Telecommunications Corp., 733 Lakefield, Westlake Village, CA 91361, 805-373-8688

Fresh Technology Group, 1478 N. Tech Blvd., #101, Gilbert, AZ 85234, 602-497-4200

Fujitsu America, Inc., 3055 Orchard Dr., San Jose, CA 95134, 408-946-8777

Fujitsu Components of America, Inc., 3320 Scott Blvd., Santa Clara, CA 95054, 408-727-1700

Funk Software, 222 Third St., Cambridge, MA 02142, 800-822-3865 (617-497-6339 in MA)

Future Soft Engineering, 1001 S. Dairy Ashford, #203, Houston, TX 77077, 713-496-9400

Future Trends Software, P.O. Box 3927, Austin, TX 78764-3927, 800-869-EASY, 512-443-6564

GammaLink, 2452 Embarcardero Way, Palo Alto, CA 94303, 415-856-7421

Gateway Communications, Inc., 2941 Alton Ave., Irvine, CA 92714, 800-367-6555 (714-553-1555 in CA)

Gems Computers, 3446 De La Cruz Blvd., Santa Clara, CA 95054, 408-988-0161

Generic Software, 11911 N. Creek Pkwy. S., Bothell, WA 98011, 800-228-3601

Golden Bow Systems, 2870 Fifth Ave., San Diego, CA 92103, 800-284-3269, 619-298-9349

GoldStar Technology, Inc., 1130 E. Arques Ave., Sunnyvale, CA 94086, 408-737-8575

Hard Drive Specialist, 16208 D Hickory Knoll, Houston, TX 77059, 800-231-6671, 713-480-6000

Haventree Software, Ltd., P.O. Box 1093-P, Thousand Island Park, NY 13692, 800-267-0668, 613-544-6035

Hayes Microcomputer Products, Inc., P.O. Box 105203, Atlanta, GA 30348, 404-449-8791

hDC Computer Corp., 15379 NE 90th St., Redmond, WA 98052, 206-885-5550

Heath Co., Hilltop Rd., St. Joseph, MI 49085, 616-982-3200

Hedge Systems, 511 W. Glen Oaks Blvd., #230, Glendale, CA 91202, 818-243-2235

Helix Software Co., Inc., 83-65 Daniels St., Briarwood, NY 11435, 800-451-0551 (718-262-8787 in NY)

Hertz Computer Corp., 325 Fifth Ave., New York, NY 10016, 800-BE-A-USER (212-684-4141 in NJ, NY, and CT)

Hewlett-Packard Co., 1820 Embarcadero Rd., Palo Alto, CA 94303, 800-752-0900

Hi-Q International, 1142 Pelican Bay Dr., Daytona Beach, FL 32019, 904-756-8988

Honeywell, 4171 N. Mesa St., El Paso, TX 79902, 915-544-5511

Houston Instruments, 8500 Cameron Rd., Austin, TX 78753, 800-444-3425, 512-835-0900

Hyundai, 800-727-6972

IBM see **International Business Machines Corp.**

IDEAssociates, Inc., 29 Dunham Rd., Billerica, MA 01821, 508-663-6878

Indigo Software, Ltd., 400-560 Rochester St., Ottawa, Canada K1S 5K2, 800-267-9976, 613-594-3026

Integrated Information Technology, Inc., 2540 Mission College Blvd., Santa Clara, CA 95054, 408-727-1885

Intel Corp., 5200 NE Elam Young Parkway, Hillsboro, OR 97124-9987, 800-538-3373

Intergraph Corp., Huntsville, AL 35894-0001, 800-345-4856 (800-345-0218 in AL)

International Business Machines Corp., 800-IBM-2468 (ask for nearest IBM dealer or sales representative)

International Computer Group, Inc., 18520 Office Park Dr., Gaithersburg, MD 20879, 800-833-2324 (301-670-7007 in MD)

Intronics Computer Corp., 1212 Knoxville St., San Diego, CA 92110, 800-422-3366, 619-276-3700

Intuit, 540 University Ave., Palo Alto, CA 94301, 800-624-8742

IQ Engineering, 586 Weddell Dr., Sunnyvale, CA 94089, 408-734-1161

Irwin Magnetic Systems, 800-BACKUP-1 (see also **Cipher Data Products, Inc.**)

C. Itoh Digital Products, Inc., 19300 S. Hamilton Ave., Torrance, CA 90502, 213-327-9100

C. Itoh Electronics, 19300 S. Hamilton Ave., Torrance, CA 90248, 213-327-9100

ITT Information Systems, 2350 Qume Dr., San Jose, CA 95131, 408-945-8950; 20 Mayfield Ave., Edison, NJ 08837, 201-225-6121

JM Systems, 1633 W. Washington Blvd., Montebello, CA 90640, 213-724-5585

Juki Office Machines Corp., 20437 S. Western Ave., Torrance, CA 90501, 800-325-6134

Kamerman Labs, 7861 SW Cirrus Dr., Beaverton, OR 97005, 800-522-2237 (503-626-6877 in AK and OR)

Kaypro Computers, 533 Stevens Ave., Solana Beach, CA 92075, 619-259-4441

Kensington Microwave, Ltd., 251 Park Ave. S., New York, NY 10010, 800-535-4242 (212-475-5200 in NY)

Key Tronic, North 4424 Sullivan Rd., Spokane, WA 99216, 509-928-8000

Kimtron Corp., 1709 Junction Ct., Bldg. 380, San Jose, CA 95112-1090, 800-828-8899

LaserGo, Inc., 9235 Trade Place, Suite A, San Diego, CA 92126, 800-451-0088, 619-530-2400

LaserMaster, 7156 Shady Oak Rd., Eden Prairie, MN 55344, 612-USA-TYPE

Lasersmith, Inc., 430 Martin Ave., Santa Clara, CA 95050, 408-727-7700

Leading Technology, Inc., 10430 SW Fifth Ave., Beaverton, OR 97005, 800-999-5323, 505-648-3424

Logitech, 6505 Kaiser Dr., Fremont, CA 94555, 800-231-7717 (800-552-8885 in CA)

Lotus Development Corp., 55 Cambridge Pkwy., Cambridge, MA 02142, 617-577-8500

Paul Mace Software, 400 Williamson Way, Ashland, OR 97520, 800-523-0258, 503-488-2322

Macola, Inc., P.O. Box 485, Marion, OH 43301-0485, 800-468-0834, 614-382-5999

Mag Computronic (USA), Inc., 17845 Skypark Circle, Suite E, Irvine, CA 92714, 714-660-8899

Magic Soft, Inc., P.O. Box 396, Lombard, IL 60148, 708-953-2374

Magnavox see **N.A.P. Consumer Electronics Corp.**

Mannesmann Tally Corp., 8301 S. 180th St., Kent, WA 98032, 206-251-5500

Manzana MicroSystems, Inc., P.O. Box 2117, Goleta, CA 93118, 805-968-1387

MathSoft, Inc., One Kendall Sq., Cambridge, MA 02139, 800-MATHCAD

Maynard Electronics, 460 E. Semoran Blvd., Casselberry, FL 32707, 800-821-8782, 407-331-6402

MECA Ventures, Inc., 355 Riverside Ave., Westport, CT 06880, 203-226-2400

Micro Display Systems, Inc., 1310 Vermillion St., P.O. Box 455, Hastings, MN 55033, 800-328-9524, 612-437-2233

Micro Express, Inc., 2114 S. Grand Ave., Santa Ana, CA 92705, 800-642-7621, 714-662-1973

Micrografx, 1303 Arapaho, Richardson, TX 75081, 800-272-3729, 214-234-1769

MicroNet, Inc., 2356 Parkside Dr., Boise, ID 83712, 208-384-9137

MicroPro, Inc., 869 Francisco Blvd., W. San Rafael, CA 94901, 800-542-7079

Micro Smart, Inc., 200 Homer Ave., Ashland, MA 01721, 800-343-8841, 617-872-9090

Microsoft Corp., 16011 NE 36th Way, Box 97017, Redmond, WA 98073-9717, 800-541-1261

Microsystems Group, 2017 Stonington, Hoffman Estates, IL 60195, 312-882-5666

Microway, P.O. Box 79, Kingston, MA 02364, 508-746-7341

Mitsuba Corp., 650 Terrace Dr., San Dimas, CA 91773, 714-592-2866

Mitsubishi Electronic America, 991 Knox St., Torrance, CA 90505, 213-515-3993, 800-556-1234 (800-441-2345 in CA)

MNC International, 2817 Anthony Ln. S., Minneapolis, MN 55418, 612-788-1099

Monitronix Corp., 929 Eastwind Dr., Suite 220, Westerville, OH 43081-3329, 614-891-3232

Motorola see **Universal Data Systems**

Mouse Systems, 47505 Seabridge Dr., Fremont, CA 94538, 415-656-1117

Multitech Systems, Inc., 82 Second Ave. SE, New Brighton, MN 55112, 612-631-3550

N.A.P. Consumer Electronics Corp., I-40 & Snow Pines Pike, P.O. Box 14810, Knoxville, TN 37914-1810, 615-521-4316

National Datacomputer, Inc., 900 Middlesex Tpke., Billerica, MA 01821, 800-346-1006, 508-663-7677

National Semiconductor, 750 Central Expy., M/S 34-10, Santa Clara, CA 95050-2627, 800-538-8510

Natural MicroSystems Corp., 8 Erie Dr., Natick, MA 01760-1313, 617-655-0700

NCR Corp., P.O. Box 785, Dayton, OH 45482-9905, 800-544-3333, 513-445-2380

NEC America, Inc., 8 Old Sod Farm Rd., Melville, NY 11747, 516-753-7000

NEC Home Electronics (USA), Inc., 1255 Michael Dr., Wood Dale, IL 60191-1094, 800-FONE-NEC, 312-860-9500

NEC Information Systems, 1414 Massachusetts Ave., Foxboro, MA 01719, 508-264-8000

Newbridge Networks Corp., 593 Herndon Pkwy., Herndon, VA 22070-5421, 800-332-1080

Newer Technology, 1117 S. Rock Rd., Suite 4, Wichita, KS 67207, 800-678-3726, 316-685-4904

Nissho Information Systems, 10855 Business Center Dr., Suite 100, Cypress, CA 90630, 800-952-1919, 714-952-8700

Peter Norton Computing, 100 Wilshire Blvd., 9th Fl., Santa Monica, CA 90401-1104, 800-365-1010

Norton-Lambert Corp., P.O. Box 4085, Santa Barbara, CA 93140, 805-964-6767

Novation, Inc., 20409 Prairie St., Box 2875, Chatsworth, CA 91311, 818-996-5060

Novell, Inc., 122 East 1700 S., Provo, UT 84606, 800-LANKIND, 801-379-5900

OCR Systems, Inc., 1800 Byberry Rd., Suite 1405, Huntingdon Valley, PA 19006, 800-233-4627

Okidata, 532 Fellowship Rd., Mt. Laurel, NJ 08054, 800-654-3282

Olivetti USA, 765 U.S. Highway 202, Somerville, NJ 08876-1289, 201-526-8200

Omnitel, 5415 Randall Pl., Fremont, CA 94538, 415-490-2202

Oracle Corp., 500 Oracle Pkwy., Redwood Shores, CA 94065, 800-ORACLE-1

Osicom Technologies, 198 Green Pond Rd., Rockaway, NJ 07866, 201-586-2550

Pacific Data Products, Inc., 6404 Nancy Ridge Dr., San Diego, CA 92121, 619-552-0880

Packard Bell, 6045 Variel Ave., Woodland Hills, CA 91367, 818-704-3905

Panasonic Industrial Co., Two Panasonic Way, Secaucus, NJ 07094, 800-222-0584

PC Designs, 5837 S. Garnette, Tulsa, OK 74146, 918-252-5550

PDS Video Technology, Inc., 1152 Santa Barbara St., San Diego, CA 92107, 619-222-7900

Peachtree Software, 4355 Shackleford Rd., Norcross, GA 30093, 800-247-3224, 404-564-5800

Penril DataComm, 207 Perry Pkwy., Gaithersburg, MD 20877-2197, 301-921-8600

Perstar Systems, Inc., 7825 E. Redfield Rd., Scottsdale, AZ 85260, 602-991-5451

PGS see **Princeton Graphic Systems**

Philips Consumer Electronics Co., 1 Philips Dr., P.O. Box 14810, Knoxville, TN 37914-1810, 615-475-0317

Practical Peripherals, Inc., 31245 La Baya Dr., Westlake Village, CA 91362, 818-991-8200

Precision Inc., 8404A Sterling St., Irving, TX 75063, 800-562-9909, 214-929-4888

Prentice Corp., 266 Caspion Dr., P.O. Box 3544, Sunnyvale, CA 94088-3544, 408-734-9810

Priam, 20 W. Montague Expwy., San Jose, CA 95134, 408-946-4600

Primetime Software, Inc., P.O. Box 27967, Santa Ana, CA 92799, 800-777-8860, 714-556-6816

Princeton Graphic Systems, 601 Ewing St., Bldg. A, Princeton, NJ 08540, 800-221-1490, 609-683-1660

Prometheus Products, Inc., 4545 Cushing Pkwy., Fremont, CA 94538, 415-490-2370

Pure Data Ltd., 200 W. Beaver Creek Rd., Richmond Hill, Ontario, Canada L4B 1B4, 416-731-6444

Quadram Corp., One Quad Way, Norcross, GA 30093-2919, 404-923-6666

Quaid Software Ltd., 45 Charles St. E., Third Floor, Toronto, Ontario, Canada M4Y 1S2, 416-961-8243

Quam Corp. see **MNC International**

Qubie, 4809 Calle Alto, Camarillo, CA 93010, 805-987-9741

Quimax Systems, Inc., 8454 Del Rey Ave., Suite 4, Sunnyvale, CA 94086, 408-773-8282

Qume Corp., 2350 Qume Dr., San Jose, CA 95131, 800-223-2479, 408-942-4000

Racal-Vadic, 1525 McCarthy Blvd., Milpitas, CA 95035, 408-432-8008

Radio Shack see **Tandy Corp./Radio Shack**

Raima Corp., 3245 146th Pl. SE, Bellevue, WA 98007, 206-747-5570

Romberg & Romberg, 6938 Briar Cove, Dallas, TX 75240, 214-934-2025

Sakata U.S.A. Corp., 651 Bonnie Ln., Elk Grove Village, IL 60007, 800-323-6647, 312-593-3211

Samsung Electronics America, Inc., 301 Mayhill St., Saddle Brook, NJ 07662, 201-587-9600

Sanyo Business Systems Corp., 51 Joseph St., Moonachie, NJ 07074, 201-440-9300

Scion Corp., 12310 Pinecrest Rd., Reston, VA 22091, 703-476-6100

Scitor Corp., 393 Vintage Park Dr., Suite 140, Foster City, CA 94404, 415-570-7700

SDI see **Software Directions, Inc.**

Seagate, P.O. Box 66360, Scotts Valley, CA 95066-0360, 800-468-DISC

Seiko Instruments USA, Inc., 1144 Ringwood Ct., San Jose, CA 95131, 800-888-0817, 408-922-5900

Sharedata, Inc., 7400 W. Detroit St., Chandler, AZ 85226, 800-BUY-INTO

Sharp Electronics Corp., Sharp Plaza, Mahwah, NJ 07430, 800-BE-SHARP, 201-529-9500

Sigma Designs, 46501 Landing Pkwy., Fremont, CA 94538, 800-933-9945

SoftLogic Solutions, Inc., One Perimeter Rd., Manchester, NH 03103, 800-272-9900 (603-627-9900 in NH)

SoftSource, 301 W. Holly, Bellingham, WA 98225, 206-676-0999

Software Directions, Inc., 1572 Sussex Tnpk., Randolph, NJ 07869, 800-346-7638 (201-584-8466 in NJ)

The Software Link, Inc., 3577 Parkway Ln., Norcross, GA 30092, 800-451-LINK, 404-448-5465

Software Publishing Corp., 1901 Landings Dr., Mountain View, CA 94039-7210, 800-345-2888, 415-962-8910

Sony Information Products Co., Sony Dr., Park Ridge, NJ 07656, 800-222-0879, 201-930-1000

Spear Technology, Inc., 710A Landwehr Rd., Northbrook, IL 60062, 312-480-7300

Sperry Corp., P.O. Box 500, Blue Bell, PA 19424, 215-542-4213

SPSS, Inc., 444 N. Michigan Ave., Chicago, IL 60611, 312-329-3316

Star Micronics America, Inc., 200 Park Ave., Suite 3510, New York, NY 10166, 212-986-6770

Sterling Software, 202 E. Airport Dr., #280, San Bernardino, CA 92408, 714-889-0226

Sunol Systems, 1177 Quarry Ln., P.O. Box 1777, Pleasanton, CA 94566, 415-484-3322

SWFTE International, Ltd., 128-B Senatorial Dr., Greenville, DE 19807, 800-237-9383 (302-429-8434 in DE)

Symantec Corp., 10201 Torre Ave., Cupertino, CA 95014, 800-228-4122, 408-253-9600

Symsoft, 444 First St., Los Altos, CA 94022, 415-941-1552

Syntrex, Inc., 41 Perimeter Center East, Atlanta, GA 30346, 800-727-8001, 201-542-1500

Sysgen, Inc., 556 Gibraltar Dr., Milpitas, CA 95035, 800-821-2151

Tallgrass Technologies Corp., 11100 W. 82nd St., Overland Park, KS 66214, 913-492-6002

Tandy Corp./Radio Shack, 1800 One Tandy Center, Fort Worth, TX 76102, 817-390-3011

Tangent Computer, Inc., 303 Beach Rd., Burlingame, CA 94010, 800-223-6677, 415-342-9388

Tatung Company of America, Inc., 2850 El Presidio St., Long Beach, CA 90810, 800-421-2929, 213-979-7055

Tave USA, Inc., 445 Park Ave., Brooklyn, NY 11205, 718-596-4100

Taxan USA Corp., 161 Nortech Pkwy., San Jose, CA 95134, 800-544-3888, 408-946-3400

Tecmar, 6225 Cochran Rd., Solon, OH 44139, 216-349-0600

Teknike Electronics Corp., 353 Rte. 46W, Fairfield, NJ 07006, 201-575-0380

Tektronix, Inc., 800-835-6100

Telenetics Corp., 895 E. Yorba Linda Blvd., Placentia, CA 92670, 714-524-5770

TeleVideo Systems, Inc., 1170 Morse Ave., Sunnyvale, CA 94086, 408-745-7760

Texas Instruments, P.O. Box 809063, Dallas, TX 75380-9063, 800-527-3500

Thomson, 5731 W. Slauson Ave., Suite 111, Culver City, CA 90230, 213-568-1002

3X USA Corp., One Executive Dr., Ft. Lee, NJ 07024, 800-327-9712 (201-592-6874 in NJ)

Toshiba of America, Inc., 2740 Irvine Blvd., Irvine, CA 92718, 800-457-7777, 714-380-3000

Touch Base Systems, Inc., 160 Laurel Ave., Northport, NY 11768, 800-541-0345 (516-261-0423 in NY)

Transcend Corp., 1887 O'Toole Ave., Suite C209, San Jose, CA 95131, 408-946-7400

Traveling Software, Inc., 18702 N. Creek Pkwy., Bothell, WA 98011, 800-662-2652, 206-483-8088

Tri-Star Computers, 1520 W. Mineral Rd., Tempe, AZ 85283, 602-838-1222

Triton Technologies, Inc., 200 Middlesex Essex Tnpk., Iselin, NJ 08830, 201-855-9440

True Basic, Inc., 12 Commerce Ave., West Lebanon, NH 03784, 800-TR-BASIC, 603-298-8517

TVM Professional Monitor Corp., 1109 W. Ninth St., Upland, CA 91786, 714-985-4788

Underware, Inc., 321 Columbus Ave., Boston, MA 02116, 800-343-7308 (617-267-9743 in MA)

UNISYS, 800-547-8362

United Software Security, Inc., 8133 Leesburg Pike, Suite 380, Vienna, VA 22182, 800-892-0007 (703-556-0007 in VA)

Universal Data Systems/Motorola, 5000 Bradford Dr., Huntsville, AL 35805-1953, 205-721-8000

USRobotics, 8100 McCormick Blvd., Skokie, IL 60076-2920, 312-982-5001

US Sage, Inc., 2005 Tree Fork Ln., Suite 125, Longwood, FL 32750, 800-999-6770, 407-331-4400

Ven-Tel, Inc., 2121 Zanker Rd., San Jose, CA 95131-2177, 800-538-5121, 408-436-7400

Victor Technologies, 380 El Pueblo Rd., Scotts Valley, CA 95066, 408-438-6680

V. I. P. C. Computers, 384 Jackson, #1, Hayward, CA 94544, 415-881-1772

VoxLink Corp., P.O. Box 23306, Nashville, TN 37202, 615-331-0275

Watcom Products, 415 Phillip St., Waterloo, Ontario, Canada N2L 3X2, 519-886-3700

Wedge Technology, Inc., 1587 McCandless Dr., Milpitas, CA 95035, 408-263-9888

Wells American Corp., 3243 Sunset Blvd., West Columbia, SC 29169, 803-796-7800

Weltec Digital, Inc., 17981 Sky Park Circle, Bldg. M, Irvine, CA 92714, 800-333-5155, 714-250-1959

Western Datacom, 5083 Market St., Youngstown, OH 44512, 800-262-3311 (212-835-1510 in OH)

WordPerfect Corp., 1555 N. Technology Way, Orem, UT 84057, 800-321-4566

Wyse Technology, 3571 N. First St., San Jose, CA 95134, 408-433-1000

WYSIWYG Corp., 300 Corporate Pointe, Suite 410, Culver City, CA 90230, 800-776-7674, 213-215-9645

Xerox Corp., 800 Salt Rd., Bldg. 843, Webster, NY 14580-9718, 800-628-2480

Xian Corp., 625 N. Monroe St., Ridgewood, NJ 07450, 201-447-3270

Xtron Computer Equipment Corp., 19 Rector St., 35th Floor, New York, NY 10006, 212-344-6583

Zenith Data Systems, 1000 Milwaukee Ave., Glenview, IL 60025, 312-699-4800

Zeos International, Ltd., 530 Fifth Ave., NW, St. Paul, MN 55112, 800-423-5891 (612-633-4591 in MN)

Zylab Corp., 3105-T N. Wilke Rd., Arlington Heights, IL 60004, 800-544-6339, 312-632-1100

Appendix B

Checklists

This Appendix provides four *checklists* to help you in the following areas:

> Needs Assessment
> Software Selection
> Hardware Selection
> Dealer Evaluation

You should use the lists as guidelines to assist you in assembling your own lists that are customized to your individual needs.

Needs Assessment

1. Use of System

Personal
Write Letters, Reports, Notes, Memos, and so forth
Maintain Address/Telephone Book
Keep Mailing List for Christmas, Birthdays, Anniversaries, and so forth
Reminder Lists
General Calendar
Other

Household
Keep Recipe and Other Card Files
Organize/Catalog Tapes, Records, Books, Collections, and so forth

Project Manager to Organize Time and Space
Enhance Home Video Productions
Computer-Controlled Timer
Computer Security System
Other

Financial
Balance a Checkbook
Budget Planner
Track/Plan/Analyze Monthly Finances
Inventory Control
Retirement, College, and Other Forecasting Analysis/Planning
Net Worth Analysis
General Assets Management
Prepare Income Tax
Other

Educational
Prepare Homework (Reports, Projects, and so forth)
Instructional Material
Drill and Practice Exercises
Learn New Things Through CAI
Prepare for Tests such as SAT, ACT, and GRE
Other

Recreational
Games
Hobbies
Draw/Paint Graphics Images
Make Greeting Cards, Large Banners, Signs, and so forth
Other

Business
Communicate with Other Computers
Report Generation
Prepare Newsletters, Bulletins, Brochures
Prepare Pie, Bar, Line, and Other Charts
Produce Slide Shows
Accounting
Sales

Payroll
Fund-raising
Other

Professional
CAD/CAM
Statistical
Data/Mathematical Analysis
Function Plotting
Equipment Control
Programming Languages
Other

Need for Support

YES	NO	1.	Are you fluent in computerese?
YES	NO	2.	Are you comfortable reading advertisements, product reports, technical specification sheets, and manuals?
YES	NO	3.	Do you have hands-on experience with a system similar to the one you are considering purchasing?
YES	NO	4.	Have you been able to obtain demonstrations for most of the major software packages that you want?
YES	NO	5.	Are you free from computerphobia?
YES	NO	6.	Do you feel you would be comfortable on your own with a new system?
YES	NO	7.	Are you a good do-it-yourselfer?
YES	NO	8.	Would you be comfortable with installing new software on your computer?
YES	NO	9.	Would you be able to troubleshoot routine system troubles?
YES	NO	10.	Could you perform routine system maintenance (such as installing new memory boards or software updates) yourself?

Needs Assessment Summary

Immediate Needs   **What to Look For**

Needs Assessment Summary (continued)

Future "Wants"   **What to Plan For**

Software Selection

Operating System
Type   Macintosh   MS-DOS   OS/2   Other _____

Other System Software
System Manager   Shell/Emulator   Utilities   Other _____

Word Processor
Features Desired   Advanced Editing/File Handling
Graphics   Thesaurus   Spell Checking   Automatic Hyphenation
Page Preview   Column Format   Outline/Index Generation
Other _____

Desktop Publisher
Features Desired   Built-in Text Editor   Clip Art Library
Import/Export of Files   Font Selection   Font Editor
Other _____

Financial Software
Checking Account Program   Budget Planner   Assets Manager
Tax Preparers   Financial Planner/Analyzer/Manager
Other _____

Spreadsheet
Features Desired   Extra Large Layouts   Import/Export of Files
Automatic Generation of Charts (Pie, Bar, Line, etc.)
Graphics   Color   Editing   Advanced Forecasting   3-D
Other _____

Household Applications

Address Book   Recipe File   Organizer   Catalog
Reminder Calendar   Project Manager   Video Production
Timer/Security   Other _____

Data Base Manager

Features Desired   Use Query Language   Import/Export of Files
Graphics   Color   Contains Report Generator   Other _____

Integrated Software

Components Desired   Word Processor   Spreadsheet
Telecommunications   Data Base Manager   Graphics
Other _____

Telecommunications Software

Will be used to access   Friend's Computer   Computer at Work
Other Microcomputers Only   A Mainframe
Electronic Bulletin Boards   Information Services
A LAN or Similar Environment   Other _____

Graphics Programs

Features Desired   Draw/Paint   Use Clip Art
Import/Export Files   Color   Generate Charts (Pie, Bar, Line, etc.)
Font Selection   Move/Size/Rotate Images   Make Slides
Other _____

Type Programs   Drawing/Painting   Sign Maker
Design Package   CAD/CAM   General Purpose
Other _____

Educational Programs

Drill and Practice   Tutorial   CAI   Instructional
Preparatory   Professional   Design   Simulations   Games
Other _____

Games

Arcade   Adventure/Fantasy/Role Playing   Mystery   Strategy
Word   Simulations   Game Shows   Sports   Card   Casino
Board   Number   Educational   Other _____

Business Packages

Comments _____

Professional Software

Comments _____

Programming Languages

BASIC   COBOL   FORTRAN   Pascal   LOGO   Forth
Prolog   Ada   ALGOL   LISP   APL   PL/1
PILOT   C   RPG   Assembly Language
Other _____

Software Selection Summary

Program Name and Version	Description and/or Type	Any Special Requirements	Product Cost

Hardware Selection

The Computer

Processor Type   _____

Coprocessor(s)   Math   Cache   Other _____

Memory Needed   _____ K

Graphics Needed   None   Macintosh   IBM   Other _____

    If IBM   Hercules   MDPA   CGA   EGA   VGA

    Other _____

Other Boards _____

Number of Slots   _____

Number of Ports   Serial _____   Parallel _____   Other _____

Upgrade Path History   Known   Unknown

    If known   Excellent   Good   Fair   Poor

Future Expansion   Memory _____ K   Number of Slots _____

    Number of Ports _____   Other_____

Data Storage

Floppy Disks   5¼ or 3½ inch? _____   DD or HD _____

    Number/Type of drives _____

Hard Disk   Size _____ MB   Speed _____ ms

    Other Features _____

Tape System   Description _____

Backup System   Tapes   Diskettes   Other _____

Keyboard

Comments _____

_____

Monitor

Screen Size   _____ inches

Type Display   Mono   Color   Composite   RGB

Other _____

Graphics (Must be compatible with computer graphics above)

Resolution   Low   Medium   High   Very High

143

Printer

Type Preferred			Dot-Matrix	Daisy-Wheel
		Ink-Jet	Laser	Typewriter
Quality	Low	Medium	High	Very High

Draft   NLQ/LQ   Daisy-Wheel   Laser   Other _____

Speed _____ cps   or _____ lpm   or _____ ppm

Pitches Needed   Pica (10 cpi)   Elite (12 cpi)
Expanded (larger than 10 cpi)
Condensed (smaller than 12 cpi)

Other _____

Fonts Needed   Roman   Orator   Courier   Gothic   Bold
Script   Bookface   Sans-Serif   Executive   OCR-A/B

Other _____

Downloadable Characters Needed   Yes   No
If Yes, is an extra buffer needed?   Yes   No

Print Enhancements   Boldface   Underline   Sub/Superscripts
Italics   Double Underline   Small Caps   Strikeout
Overprint   Other _____

Color Needed   Yes   No
If Yes, number of colors   _____

Graphics Needed   Yes   No
If Yes, resolution needed   Low   Medium   High   Very High

Carriage Width   Standard   Wide

Tractor Needed   Yes   No
If Yes   Rear Feed   Bottom Feed

Sheet Feeder Needed   Yes   No
If Yes   One Bin   Two Bins   Three Bins   Other _____

Modem

Transmission Rate   300   1200   2400   Other _____ baud
Automatic Modes   AA/AD   Other _____
Compatibility _____

Other Input/Output Devices

Cartridges   Joysticks   Mouse   Track Ball   Light Pen
Graphics Tablet   Plotter   Scanner
Voice Recognition System   Sound/Speech Synthesizer
Other _____

_____

Protection and Convenience Devices

Dust Covers   Glare Screen   Monitor Turntable   Printout Basket
Sound Baffle for Printer   Static Guards   Power Conditioners
Power Strips/Directors   Uninterruptable Power Supply   Other _____

Cables
Comments _____

Documentation
Comments _____

Support and Service
Comments _____

Computer Furniture
Comments _____

Hardware Selection Summary

Brand/Model of Component	Description and/or Type	Any Special Requirements	Product Cost

Dealer Evaluation

Dealer Name _____

Description _____

Part 1 Reputation and Reliability

YES	NO	1.	Is the store clean, neat, and well arranged?
YES	NO	2.	Do you have personal knowledge or independent assurance that the dealer has a good reputation?
YES	NO	3.	Has the dealer been in business more than three years?
YES	NO	4.	Is the dealer listed with the Better Business Bureau with no unresolved complaints?
YES	NO	5.	If you have requested them, were references available?

Part 2 General Information

YES	NO	6.	Are the salespersons helpful?
YES	NO	7.	Are any demonstrations that you need available?
YES	NO	8.	Do you feel that the salespeople are being honest with you?
YES	NO	9.	Do you feel that the salespeople are knowledgeable and competent?
YES	NO	10.	Are prices competitive?
YES	NO	11.	Are prices clearly and freely stated?
YES	NO	12.	Are most of the items you want in stock for immediate delivery?
YES	NO	13.	Will training be available if you need it?
YES	NO	14.	Will adequate post-purchase support be available?
YES	NO	15.	Does this dealer provide service?

Appendix C

Ratings of Laptop Computers
(IBM-PC Compatible)

Miniaturizing a computer once meant compromising it with hard-to-read screens, inadequate keyboards, limited expansion capabilities, and astronomical prices. Few people outside the business world could justify the expense or put up with the limitations of the downsized package.

Now, laptop screens and keyboards have been improved even as prices have dropped.

Laptops are not confined to lap use: A portable computer light enough for the lap is also light enough to move from room to room, to take on trips, and for students to carry easily from dorm to library and back home on vacations.

A typical laptop weighs 10 to 12 pounds, batteries included. Figure an extra pound or two for the AC adapter, which runs the machine on house current. That sounds light, but anyone who has carried one of these machines from one end of an airport to another will appreciate why the future of miniaturized computing lies in even smaller machines. To get an idea what's coming, see pages 157–58 for information on two notebook-sized computers.

Laptop Details

Keyboards are especially idiosyncratic, both in how they're laid out and how the keys feel. What the hunt-and-peck typist may find quite all right, the touch typist may dislike.

Here are other things to consider:

The Screen Early laptops used a reflective liquid crystal display, or LCD, similar to the display found on digital watches. Reflective screens depend greatly on the quality of the ambient light; in some light, you can read the screen only when it's angled just right. Some units still use a reflective screen, although in an improved version called "super twist." It shows blue letters against a silvery background.

The next step forward was the backlit LCD screen, which supplies its own light from a gray or silvery fluorescent light source, resulting in much more brightness and contrast. One still has to adjust the screen angle to see it properly, however, and the blue letters aren't as crisp as what you'd see on a first-class monitor. But the better backlit designs are quite readable.

More advanced technologies have found their way into the most expensive laptops. One, called gas plasma, produces a very crisp orange-on-black image that some have likened to a neon light. It uses so much power, though, that gas-plasma laptops don't run on batteries.

Screen Size A laptop displays the full 25 lines and 80 characters that a regular cathode-ray tube monitor shows. Some greatly compress the letters to keep the screen short. Others stretch the letters to fill a squarer screen. Graphics show best on squarer screens.

Display Format Laptop displays, though monochromatic, typically use the same video display protocol as that used for medium-resolution color graphics displays, a format called CGA. These laptops can run programs that use graphic elements such as pie charts, bar graphs, and the like, in addition to producing easily readable text.

When running programs that make use of color, the laptops substitute shades of gray. This gray scale should be adequate for most uses. In case it isn't, laptops generally have an RGB port for plugging in a color monitor to substitute for the LCD screen. You might want to use that for certain programs that make heavy use of color.

Some laptop designs allow the addition of higher-resolution color display formats, such as EGA, for use with an external monitor.

Memory Laptops usually come with a generous amount of temporary memory, or RAM. Most come with 640K, enough to use just about any program the MS-DOS operating system can normally access, including most heavyweight business programs. Some computers either come with or can be outfitted with extended RAM memories of 1,200K or more, which allows various software-speeding techniques such as "disk-caching" and the creation of "RAM disks."

Disk Drives The standard floppy disk drive for laptops has become a 3½-inch microfloppy, the same as that used by the *IBM-PS2* line of computers and the *Apple Macintosh*. Such floppies typically have a capacity of 720K apiece, equivalent to roughly 360 pages of typed text.

One such drive might be enough for the simpler computer tasks, such as ordinary word processing or spreadsheet work. But two drives are more convenient.

A floppy and a hard disk drive are more convenient still. Hard drives hold much more information than floppies and can thus handle more complex, bulkier programs. And they're significantly faster.

Unfortunately, a 20-megabyte hard drive, available in most laptop lines, comes at a high price. Business users may consider the expense worthwhile.

Data Transfer   People who use a desktop computer either at home or at the office may need to transfer documents between the laptop and the machine from time to time. But since most desktops use 5¼-inch floppy disks, that's not so simple. There are two common solutions to the problem. The first is to use a so-called bridge program. With one type, you cable the machines together using a serial port and run the bridge program on both machines. The program transfers your documents, formats intact.

A simpler solution is either to outfit the desktop with a 3½-inch disk drive or buy an external 5¼-inch floppy drive for the laptop and copy from one drive to another. Laptops have a port for an external disk drive. Adding such a drive costs about $200 to $300.

Modems, which connect computers via telephone lines, can also be used to transfer data from laptop to desktop. Laptops can generally be equipped with an internal modem for $100 to $200 extra.

Speed

Computation speed depends on two things: the silicon chip at the heart of the laptop and the "clock speed," measured in megahertz, at which the computer runs. Some laptops are equipped with the 8088 chip typical of IBM and IBM-compatible XT-level computers. Others have more advanced chips, such as the 8086 or the *NEC V20* or *V30*.

For ordinary word processing and many other uses, however, computation speed is of minor importance (disk speed matters more). For routine word-processing tasks, most people won't notice the speed differences between one computer and another.

Battery Power

Battery life is most important for those who must compute where AC power is not available—in a classroom, on a plane, or out in the backyard. If you need a machine that's just portable enough to take from home to office and back, battery life is of less interest.

In a Consumers Union test, each laptop was adjusted to its brightest screen setting and ran a complex word-processing routine that kept a disk drive running 10 percent of the time.

One model, with a battery about twice as heavy as the others, ran 5½ hours, while another could manage less than 3 hours. One laptop without a battery-taxing illuminated screen also ran a long time: 5¼ hours. (Hard drives, like backlit screens, use extra power, so batteries don't last as long in hard-drive laptops as they do in floppy-drive machines.)

If one were planning to use battery power for extended periods, one could purchase extra battery packs, but that's not an option with some models whose batteries are wired in.

A "low battery" warning light gives you time to save your work before the battery conks out completely.

Recommendations

Laptop computers offer all the essential computer functions in small, sometimes very well designed packages. But in deciding about buying a laptop, you must judge whether portability and compactness are worth several hundred dollars, for that's the price differential between a laptop and a comparable desktop IBM clone.

RATINGS

Listed in order of estimated quality, based on performance and convenience. Differences of 5 or more points in overall score are significant. Screen judgments assess readability; keyboard judgments, convenience of the layout. Portability is a combination of weight, bulk, and handle design. Speed is based on a series of software tests. As published in a September 1989 report.

Toshiba T1200FB
$2199

Altogether, the best combination of portability and usefulness, in a package that weighs just under 10 pounds. The backlit screen is the clearest and easiest to read of any laptop in the group.

One of the *Toshiba*'s many noteworthy features is Resume, a circuit linked to an auxiliary battery that backs up the computer's RAM memory. When you turn off the machine, Resume keeps the memory intact for up to 20 hours. You can then take up where you left off, without having to start the program from scratch.

The disk drives (two floppies on the "F" models, one floppy and one hard drive on the "H" models) are located conveniently on one side of the machine. (The hard-drive model costs about $500 more.) The keyboard, while compact, still has separate Home, Page Up, Page Down, and End keys, as well as an oversized Backspace key. Other features include a "battery charged" light and a port for an external numeric keypad—a must if you do a lot of number-crunching. There's room to add a high-resolution EGA color-video display card, should you need the crisp color that an EGA monitor can provide. The keyboard lacks a Caps Lock light, a minor inconvenience.

Score: 87
Screen　　　　●
Portability　　◑
Speed　　　　●
Keyboard　　　◑
RAM: 1000K, expandable to 2000K
Battery life: 3 hrs.
Weight with battery: 9.9 lbs.
Weight of AC adapter: 1.2 lbs.

NEC Multispeed EL-2
$2499

The *NEC*'s display has the best contrast in the group and is very readable, though not quite up to the level of the *Toshiba T1200*. Like all backlit screens, it emits a slight buzz. Usually you'll notice the buzz only in a quiet room. This buzz, however, is a bit louder.

The two disk drives are placed, conveniently, on the right-hand edge. The keyboard features a separate numeric keypad, but it and the cursor keys are in a nonstandard position, at the upper right. Ten function keys are conveniently arrayed on the left side. There is no light to indicate that the battery is charging.

Score: 79
Screen　　　　◑
Portability　　○
Speed　　　　●

Keyboard ◐
RAM size: 640K, not expandable
Battery life: 3¼ hrs.
Weight with battery: 11.7 lbs.
Weight of AC adapter: 2.5 lbs.

Epson Equity LT
$2847

At 13 pounds, the *Epson* is one of the heavier and bulkier laptops. Part of that size is to accommodate a large keyboard with one of the best layouts around. It has oversized Backspace and Return keys and a separate numeric keypad, so it's a good choice for those who work with numbers. Unfortunately, the keys don't travel far enough to feel as precise as some may wish.

The *Epson*'s two disk drives are placed one on each side of the unit, a small inconvenience, and they were a tad noisy. If you may use a hard drive someday, it pays to decide before you buy: The unit can be upgraded later with a hard disk drive for $900, while *Epson*'s hard-drive laptop costs about an extra $500. The built-in battery is not removable, so you can't take along extra battery packs if you need to work for long periods away from an AC outlet. Unlike the other designs, there's no separate port for an external drive, leaving just one parallel port for use by a printer, external disk drive, or other peripheral equipment. Epson also sells versions with a reflective screen that list for about $1000 less.

Score: 78
Screen ◐
Portability ◖
Speed ◉
Keyboard ◉
RAM: 640K, not expandable
Battery life: 2¾ hrs.
Weight with battery: 13 lbs.
Weight of AC adapter: 1.7 lbs.

Tandy (Radio Shack) 1400LT
$1799

Tandy, a laptop pioneer with its notebook-sized *Model 100,* has taken a more conventional approach with the *1400LT,* a heavy, fairly bulky IBM-compatible machine. One desirable feature is its two disk drives mounted just back of the keyboard, within easy reach. Folding the screen down protects them from the elements. The very readable screen has a contrast adjustment but no brightness control. You can turn the backlighting off from the keyboard. The keyboard is the quietest in the group, has a good feel to it, and features oversized Backspace and Return keys. A numeric keypad is embedded, but there's a port for a full-sized keyboard if you wish to add one.

The *1400LT* lacks a light that indicates the battery is charging.

Score: 74
Screen:　　　◓
Portability　◓
Speed　　　◓
Keyboard　　◉
RAM: 768K, not expandable
Battery life: 4¾ hrs.
Weight with battery: 13.4 lbs.
Weight of AC adapter: 1.2 lbs.

Datavue Spark
$995

A small, lightweight machine, the *Spark* would seem to lend itself to use by students and others interested in basic, medium-duty computing. One with a 720K disk drive suits that need but may have to be special-ordered. Buying that way can result in a price that's the same as a two-drive model.

The *Spark*'s disk drive lacks any kind of door flap, so its innards are exposed to the elements. The screen display has a contrast adjustment but no brightness control. That drawback is somewhat mitigated by a keyboard control that enables you to alter the palette, or choice of gray shades, displayed on-screen by a program. You can also turn off the backlighting from the keyboard. The screen itself may be a little flimsy on some samples, tending to flop over instead of staying put in the angle that's best for viewing. A couple of nice features: The machine beeps if you close the cover without turning it off, to help prevent running down the battery by mistake. And you can change the cursor from an underline to a block, to see it better.

The keys are set farther back on the keyboard than on other units, and there are no lights on the Shift Lock and Number Lock keys.

You may have to pay extra for the machine's battery pack, and a hard-disk upgrade costs an additional $700.

Score: 72
Screen   O
Portability   ◒
Speed   ◒
Keyboard   O
RAM: 640K, not expandable
Battery life: 3½ hrs.
Weight with battery: 9.7 lbs.
Weight of AC adapter: 1.2 lbs.

Datavue Snap
$2395

The *Snap* has an odd feature somewhat reminiscent of a transformer toy: The keyboard-and-screen unit separates from the battery-and-disk-drive part of the machine, creating an ultra-portable computer without disk drives. However, the divided machine is not usable unless you snap in an $1195 memory board, which also supplies battery power. This half-computer doesn't have much usefulness.

Where the *Snap* comes into its own is in its regular, fully assembled configuration. The rear half of the unit has two disk drives, one on either side, and a standard half-width IBM expansion slot. One use for that slot could be adding a high-resolution video-display card. That way one can substitute a high-resolution EGA or VGA color monitor for the LCD screen display and use programs that depend on sharp, colorful graphics. One could alternatively use the slot to add a monochrome editor board or any other half-sized add-on board.

Readability is good, though not the best.

It has no brightness control per se, but, like the *Spark,* the *Snap* can be cycled through a palette of foreground-background gray shades to find a good contrast, and it allows the cursor shape to be changed. The backlighting can be shut off from the keyboard.

The keyboard has a separate numeric keypad, but it and the cursor keys are placed rather inconveniently at the upper right. There are no lights on the Shift Lock and Number Lock keys. As with the *Spark,* you may have to pay extra for the battery.

Score: 71
Screen   O
Portability   ◒

Speed   ◓

Keyboard   ○

RAM: 640K, expandable to 1640K

Battery life: 3½ hrs.

Weight with battery: 11.7 lbs.

Weight of AC adapter: 2 lbs.

Zenith SupersPort 184-1
$2399

The *Zenith*'s screen, which measures 6 by 8 inches, is the largest in the group, a small advantage in displaying graphics, less of one when displaying text. However, the screen isn't as bright as some other machines', and the text display is thus not as readable in bright light as it might be. The grays can be adjusted from the keyboard.

The keyboard has a fine layout, with an oversized Return key. The numeric keypad is embedded, but there is a port to accommodate an external keypad. The two disk drives are a bit inconveniently located, one on each side. The batteries in the *SupersPort* should last longer than any of the others, not so surprising when you consider that its battery weighs at least twice as much as other laptop batteries. Altogether, it's one of the heavier machines.

The *SupersPort* also comes in a hard-drive version, the *184-2*, that runs $1200 more. Adding a hard disk later will cost about $1700.

Score: 71

Screen   ○

Portability ○

Speed   ◓

Keyboard   ◉

RAM: 640K, expandable to 1640K

Battery life: 5½ hrs.

Weight with battery: 12.5 lbs.

Weight of AC adapter: 1.5 lbs.

Toshiba T1000
$999

The *Toshiba T1000*, set up with one disk drive, is a fairly rudimentary computer. But its low price, good keyboard, and extreme portability (a shade over 6 pounds) make it a reasonable choice for a college student or other person interested in light- to medium-duty computing on the go.

The *T1000*'s big drawback is that it has a plain, reflective LCD screen. Text is readable but lacks brightness. Also, the display is only 3 inches high. While it still shows 25 lines of text in that space, characters look a little squashed. The screen so dims the other shining virtues of the machine that a small business has sprung up in retrofitting *T1000*s with backlit screens ($295 from Axonix, Salt Lake City, Utah, 801-466-9797).

Though the keyboard is a little more cramped than the *T1200*'s, it still has a good layout, with an oversized Backspace key and separate Home, Page Up, Page Down, and End keys. The numeric keypad is embedded, but there's a port for adding an external keypad. There are no lights to indicate battery charging, Caps Lock, or Number Lock.

The built-in battery isn't removable, but since battery life was a respectable 5¼ hours in Consumers Union's tests, that shouldn't be a real drawback most of the time.

Score: 65
Screen   ●
Portability   ◑
Speed   ○
Keyboard   ◕
RAM: 512K, expandable to 1280K
Battery life: 5¼ hrs.
Weight with battery: 6.2 lbs.
Weight of AC adapter: 1.3 lbs.

Tiny Laptops

The *Cambridge Z88* weighs just under 3 pounds, has a full-sized keyboard, comes with built-in software, and sells for just $450. Unfortunately, the *Z88* is far from the IBM world.

The *Z88* uses a processor chip and operating system fundamentally incompatible with those of an IBM-type computer. There are no disk drives and hence no library of software to choose from. You use instead the built-in software, which has as its centerpiece a combination word processor and spreadsheet called *Pipedream*. Work output is held in RAM memory, backed up with a rechargeable battery that is said to keep the RAM intact for up to a year. The rest of the machine runs on four AA cells.

The RAM that comes standard with the machine is just 32K, but most of that is used up by the software, leaving room for only a few pages of text. Adding more RAM is virtually mandatory. You can get a 32K RAM cartridge for $45 (allowing about 16 extra pages) or a 128K card for $110 (about 64 pages). Obviously, the *Z88* is for note-taking, not for novel writing.

Pipedream has all the rudimentary word-processor and spreadsheet functions, but it works quite unlike other programs. For instance, the word processor and spreadsheet are both active simultaneously. One result is that the word processor lacks a tab function, which is given over to the spreadsheet part of the program. You can print documents using the *Cambridge*'s single serial port and an *Epson*-compatible printer. The screen, a reflective LCD type, needs bright ambient lighting to be viewable. The keyboard and screen are in the same plane—but the angle that's best for viewing, roughly 45 degrees, is not best for typing. Further, the screen displays a mere six lines of text, 72 to 99 columns wide, and the characters are quite small. The keyboard is covered with a soft rubber overlay, and the keys travel only a short distance. While it takes only a light touch to hit a key, the keyboard has a toylike typing feel.

Getting *Z88* documents saved onto disks can be tedious. One way is through the computer's built-in terminal software, which sends documents (in a stripped-down ASCII version) via cable to other computers.

Alternatively, you can buy link kits to transfer documents to *Apple Macintosh* or *IBM PC* computers. The $75 *PC LINK II* kit converts *Pipedream* documents to *Wordstar* or *Lotus 1-2-3* files. That's fine for *Wordstar* and *Lotus* users, but people who use other word processors or spreadsheets may have to run another conversion program to make the files into something else.

If a computer has good programs of its own and if it's the only computer you use, you needn't insist on IBM compatibility (ask any *Apple Macintosh* user). But the *Cambridge*'s inadequate memory, screen display, keyboard, and data-storage features put this machine beyond serious consideration for the average user. It would work best as a notebook adjunct for someone who works mainly on another machine.

Tiny but Expensive

The *NEC UltraLite* is a sleek black box about the size of a slim notebook, with a weight of 4¼ pounds. Its lid opens to reveal a full-sized, backlit LCD screen and a low-profile keyboard with cursor keys at the lower left. Screen readability would be considered fairly good for a moderately priced laptop, but the *UltraLite* is not moderately priced. At a cost of $2795, plus another $325 for an external 3½-inch floppy disk drive, it is expensive.

The external drive is a must because the *NEC*, like the *Cambridge*, has no built-in drive of its own. In lieu of disks the *NEC* has two megabytes (2000K) of RAM memory, backed up by an auxiliary battery, that acts as a solid-state disk. The machine also has 640K of conventional RAM memory and a built-in modem. To use the machine, one loads a program from an external drive into the RAM disk. The program and any data you create is held there for up to a week between recharges.

While the *UltraLite* uses an advanced version of the *IBM PC XT*'s processor chip, it runs quite a lot faster than other similar machines in operations that access the disk frequently. On the whole, it runs as fast as the best of the other laptops.

The *UltraLite* has the MS-DOS operating system software built in, as well as a built-in file-transfer program, which can be used in lieu of the external drive for moving your data and programs from or to another computer. The process of transferring data is a little cumbersome, though. It's probably easier just to use an external drive.

After 90 minutes of use a warning light alerts you to another half-hour of running time. While that's a good safety margin, the battery doesn't last long enough to sustain a work session for even a medium-length airplane ride.

NEC has done a fine job of packing an IBM computer into a neat 4-pound package. But with no built-in disk, a merely good display, a cramped if adequate keyboard, and short battery life, the *UltraLite* won't satisfy a mainstream computer user. The *UltraLite* makes a nice conversation piece but an expensive one.

Mini-Dictionary

This list provides definitions for the terms most commonly used with microcomputers and their accessories, including hardware, software, and applications. If more than one term is frequently associated with the same item or concept, each is listed with a reference to the most common or preferred usage. Related terms have been carefully cross-referenced. Many of the abbreviations and acronyms used in computer terminology are also explained.

A

AA/AD   see **auto-answer** and **auto-dial.**

access   to store or retrieve data from a storage device such as a disk or tape.

access arm   a device that holds and moves the read/write heads to the proper position on a disk system.

access time   the time required to locate a specific position on a storage device such as a disk or tape in order to store or retrieve data. For a disk, this is the sum of the seek time and rotational delay.

acoustic coupler   older terminology for a modem used to connect a computer to a telephone for telecommunications.

acoustic enclosure   see **sound baffle.**

acronym   a word made by taking the first letters or few letters from the words of a phrase or name. As examples, see **ANSI, COBOL, EAROM,** and **FORTRAN.**

actuator   a device that produces action such as an access arm.

A/D   see **A to D conversion.**

address 1. the location of a specific value in main memory or on auxiliary storage. 2. to send data to a specific location.

ADP abbreviation for **automated data processing.**

AI abbreviation for **artificial intelligence:** 1. the study of computer systems capable of simulating human thought and reasoning. 2. the simulation of human reasoning and thought by a computer.

algorithm a specific set of instructions for accomplishing a certain task, stated in a definite number of steps.

alphabetic containing only the letters of the alphabet.

alphameric same as **alphabetic.**

alphanumeric containing the letters of the alphabet and/or the ten digits 0 to 9.

ALU abbreviation for **arithmetic/logic unit,** the part of the CPU that contains the circuits to perform all arithmetic and logical operations.

analog characterized by the direct representation of the measurement of continuous quantities such as speed, length, voltage, temperature, and intensity. Analog data is stored as signals, the strength of which is proportional to the size of the corresponding data values. See also **digital.**

analog computer an electronic device designed to accept and process analog data without converting it to digital format. These are usually special-purpose computers designed for scientific or engineering applications. See also **digital computer.**

ANSI (an-see) acronym for **A**merican **N**ational **S**tandards **I**nstitute, an independent organization that researches and establishes standards in many areas, not just computers.

application software programs written to accomplish a particular task for the user of a computer. See also **procedure-oriented, user-oriented,** and **system software.**

architecture structure and design of a CPU or computer system.

archival storage the offline storage of information that is not presently required but may be needed for possible future reference. See also **auxiliary storage.**

arithmetic/logic unit see **ALU.**

arithmetic operation any operation involving the addition, subtraction, multiplication, or division of numeric data.

array an ordered list or arrangement. See also **table.**

artificial intelligence see **AI.**

ASCII (ask-ee) acronym for **A**merican **S**tandard **C**ode for **I**nformation **I**nterchange. This 7-bit code for data storage was originally developed by ANSI for use by terminals to establish a common format in telecommunications. It has since evolved into an 8-bit code used by most modern computers including nearly all microcomputers. See also **EBCDIC.**

assembler   a program that translates a source program written in assembly language into an object program in machine language that can be executed by the computer. See also **compiler** and **interpreter.**

assembly language   a low-level programming language that makes use of mnemonic codes to represent operations and values such as ADD for the add operation or P for payment. Assembly language programs are rarely portable between different types of computers. See also **assembler** and **high-level language.**

asynchronous   characterized by irregularly timed operations that are usually preceded by a start signal and followed by a stop signal. See also **synchronous.**

AT   a powerful IBM PC.

A to D conversion   the conversion of data or signals from analog to digital format. See also **D to A conversion** and **modem.**

auto-answer   the mode offered by many modems in which they automatically answer the phone for incoming calls. The telecommunications software must also support this feature.

auto-dial   the mode offered by many modems in which they automatically dial the phone for outgoing calls. The telecommunications software must also support this feature.

auxiliary storage   a method of data storage in which data is stored outside of the computer's main memory but still online and ready for use as needed. The most common type used with microcomputers is a disk system. See also **archival storage** and **main memory.**

B

background process   a relatively low priority process that is performed when the CPU is free from other processing duties.

backup   1. a copy or procedure to be used in the event of the loss of the original. 2. to make or set up a backup.

backup file   a copy of a file saved in case the original is lost or damaged.

backup system   a procedure used to maintain a current copy or otherwise secure against the loss of the important online data in case all or any part is damaged or destroyed. See also **grandfather system.**

backward compatibility   the ability of a new product to properly work with other products that use older technology.

bar code   a method for input of data that makes use of a series of usually parallel bars of varying widths and spacing. See also **UPC.**

base memory   see **conventional memory.**

BASIC   acronym for **B**eginner's **A**ll-purpose **S**ymbolic **I**nstruction **C**ode, a high-level programming language designed to be easy to learn and use, and one that is considered an excellent first language. BASIC is the most common programming language found and used on microcomputers.

Basic Input/Output System   the part of a disk operating system that controls the input of data to and output of information from the CPU.

batch file   a file that causes batch processing to occur.

batch processing   a method whereby a series of programs are submitted to the system to be executed in a sequence. Although most processing on microcomputers is performed interactively, many systems provide batch file capability. See also **interactive processing.**

baud   a measure of data transfer rate, practically speaking, 1 bit per second. Thus, data transferred at the rate of 1,200 bits every second is equivalent to 1,200 baud, or about 15 words per second.

BDOS   (bee-dos) acronym for **B**asic **D**isk **O**perating **S**ystem. See **DOS.**

benchmark   a relative measure of performance. Computers can be compared by running the same program and comparing the results for such things as execution speed.

benchmark program   a computer program designed to perform a benchmark test.

Bernoulli box   an external disk storage device commonly (but not necessarily) used in networks.

bidirectional printer   a character printer that prints in two, usually alternating directions to increase printing speed. One line is printed from left to right and the next from right to left.

binary digit   one of the two numbers (0 and 1) used in the binary number system.

binary number system   the number system based on the number 2. It has only two digits, 0 and 1, which makes it very useful for representing digital values in computer storage as present (1) or absent (0). Binary numbers are sometimes indicated by a subscript of 2 such as 1001110_2. See also **decimal number system, hexadecimal number system,** and **octal number system.**

BIOS   (bye-ose) acronym for **B**asic **I**nput/**O**utput **S**ystem.

bit   a contraction for **b**inary dig**it**.

bit-mapping   addressing each pixel (dot) on a CRT screen individually.

This is essential for anything other than very low resolution graphics. See also **block-mapping.**

block a group of bytes or words treated as a unit for data storage and input/output operations to and from the storage device. Using blocks saves storage space and reduces access time. See also **page.**

block-mapping addressing as a single unit a group of pixels such as those required to produce a single character on a CRT screen. This is the method used by most computers for the display of standard text as in word processing. See also **bit-mapping.**

BNC connector a coaxial design connector sometimes used with a monitor cable.

board a unit on which various electronic components are mounted. Boards may contain anything from chips to other boards and normally have connectors along the edge for attaching to circuit elements or other boards. See also **card, integrated circuit, motherboard,** and **printed circuit board.**

boot to bring a system into operation. This normally involves loading part or all of the operating system into main memory from auxiliary storage or a ROM chip. See also **bootstrap, cold boot,** and **warm boot.**

bootable disk a disk containing the bootstrap that can be used to boot the system.

bootstrap the part of the operating system that must be loaded into main memory in order to bring the system into operation.

boot track the section of a disk that contains the bootstrap.

bpi abbreviation for **bits per inch,** a measure of the data density of a tape or disk.

bps abbreviation for **bits per second,** a measure of data transfer rate. See also **baud.**

buffer a memory area used to hold data temporarily while it is being transferred from one location or device to another. Buffers are essential for the efficient operation of the CPU and are often used in printers and other output devices to compensate for differences in processing speed.

bug an error in a computer program.

bulletin board see **electronic bulletin board.**

burst 1. to separate continuous forms into single sheets. 2. a continuous stream of data on a data communications channel.

bus circuits that provide an electronic interface to permit communication between two devices, usually the CPU and another unit.

bus network a system of two or more PCs connected by a single cable and able to communicate with one another. Only one computer needs to run the software that makes the network function. See also **LAN, ring network,** and **star network.**

byte   the basic storage unit needed to store a single character, most frequently 8 bits.

C

C   a high-level programming language especially useful for system software development.

cache memory   a high-speed data storage that acts as a buffer between the microprocessor and main memory.

CAD   acronym for **C**omputer-**A**ided **D**esign, programs or entire systems that teach or assist in the development of projects in design-related fields such as drafting, architecture, and engineering. See also **CAM.**

CADAM   sometimes used for **CAD/CAM.**

CAD/CAM   a combined CAD and CAM system. Such systems can be very powerful in precision design and project planning that require great detail.

CADD   acronym for **C**omputer-**A**ided **D**esign and **D**rawing. See **CAD.**

CAI   abbreviation for **computer-assisted instruction.** These packages are designed to provide eductional training either as stand-alone units or as supplements to other materials. They are available in nearly every field and at any level.

calculator   a device used to execute mathematical operations but usually with manual direction and operation of each step.

CAM   acronym for **C**omputer-**A**ided **M**anufacturing, programs or entire systems for the development of manufacturing design projects ranging from precision machine parts to intricate electronic circuits. See also **CAD.**

canned program   a prepared set of computer instructions supplied by a vendor in machine-readable format that may be executed but not examined or changed in any way by the user.

card   a printed circuit board that is designed to serve a particular function, such as additional memory or grapics, and normally is designed to easily plug in or otherwise connect to the system. See also **board** and **chip.**

cathode ray tube   see **CRT.**

cell   1. a unit of storage as for a single character. 2. a position for an entry on a spreadsheet.

central processing unit   see **CPU.**

Centronics port   a common type of parallel port used by most microcomputers. Printers for IBM-compatible computers most frequently make use of the Centronics port. See also **RS-232-C port.**

CGA card IBM's **Color/Graphics Adapter,** an older color graphics board for its PCs. See also **EGA card, Hercules Card, MDPA card,** and **VGA card.**

channel 1. a path for the transfer of data. 2. a track on a tape.

character graphics a system of graphics display that generates images from a specified set of graphics characters. The number of such characters is limited, and additional shapes can be made only by combining the available ones in creative ways.

character printer a device that prints one character at a time. Also known as a serial printer. See also **line printer** and **page printer.**

character set the letters and symbols supported by a particular system or software package. The set may consist of only the letters of the alphabet (upper- and lowercase), the ten digits (0–9), and special symbols, such as punctuation marks (the common ASCII 96-character set), or it may include graphics characters as well.

check bit see **parity bit.**

chip an integrated circuit commonly used for the microprocessor and memory of a microcomputer.

clip art prepared graphics images that can be incorporated into a document using a program such as a word processor or desktop publisher.

clock a circuit in the CPU that times all processes by comparing them to a set frequency. See also **clock speed.**

clock/calendar part of a computer system that automatically keeps track of the current date and time. It is usually provided on a microcomputer as a battery-powered expansion board.

clock speed the rate at which the CPU clock operates, usually measured in megahertz (MHz). In theory, the faster the clock speed, the faster the CPU will perform its operations. Most microcomputers now work at clock speeds ranging from 1 MHz to over 25 MHz.

clone a copy.

chroma the color part of a video signal. See also **luma** and **separated composite.**

coaxial cable a type of connection used for telecommunications that can carry more data than conventional telephone lines.

COBOL acronym for **CO**mmon **B**usiness **O**riented **L**anguage, a high-level language developed primarily for programming applications related to business problems.

code 1. a set of instructions such as a program. 2. to write a program.

3. one or more characters that perform a specific function such as a control code. 4. a scheme for the representation of data such as ASCII and EBCDIC.

cold boot   to start up a system that has been shut down. Sometimes this can be simulated by pressing a set of keys on the keyboard or a Reset button that clears the main memory and reloads the bootstrap. But even this does not always work, and the computer may have to be turned off to get a true cold boot. See also **warm boot.**

collate   to combine two files in a specified order into a single file in the same order.

COM   acronym for **computer output to microfilm.**

command   an instruction, usually entered directly from the keyboard, to cause some action to occur. For example, the simple command DIR would cause the computer to list on the screen all the files in the current directory or on the active disk.

command file   a program file that permits the program to be run by simply entering a single command such as the program name.

communications protocol   the signals necessary to transmit data across a data communications channel. See also **protocol.**

compiler   a program that translates a source program written in a high-level language into an object program in machine language, which then must be executed (possibly after additional processing). The process usually includes an examination of the program for errors and a listing of the associated diagnostics. See also **assembler** and **interpreter.**

composite video   a video input similar to regular television that is normally suitable for most 40-column monochrome text displays and low-resolution color graphics. See also **RGB video.**

compressed format   1. see **condensed mode.** 2. a method of data storage that eliminates all unnecessary and redundant bits.

computer   an electronic device capable of receiving instructions and data, performing the indicated logic and arithmetic operations at high speed, and issuing the result. All computers consist of the same basic components: the ALU, the control unit, main memory, and input/output devices. (Nearly all also have at least one auxiliary storage device, but this is not necessary to the basic function of a computer.)

computer-aided design   see **CAD.**

computer-aided manufacturing   see **CAM.**

computer-assisted instruction   see **CAI.**

computerese   slang for the special terminology or language used by those who work with computers. It is characterized by the use of a large number of acronyms and abbreviations. For example, see **ASCII, DOS,** and **RAM.**

computer literacy the study of computers in order to acquire the basic understanding and knowledge needed to be able to communicate and work with them.

computer output to microfilm a system that directs the output image to microfilm. This is particularly useful when large quantities of information are to be produced and stored, because it requires much less space than storing the same data on paper.

computerphobia the fear of computers.

computer program a program or set of instructions written in such a way that it can be entered into and executed by a computer.

computer programming language a language designed to permit the construction of a program that can be entered into and executed by a computer.

concatenate to link together into a single unit. For example, if the files that contain the chapters of a report are placed together end to end, they form a single *concatenated* file.

condensed mode printing small or reduced characters usually in the range of 15 to 20 characters per inch. Not only does this allow more characters to be printed on a line, but it also permits a standard carriage printer to simulate outputs from a wide carriage model.

configuration the design or way the various components of a computer system are connected or linked together. This normally refers not only to the way the hardware is physically connected together but also to how the software is set up to govern the computer and its peripherals.

connect time the duration that a terminal is actually connected to a computer. See also **CPU time.**

context sensitive responsive to a specific item or situation. For example, many software packages now come with *context sensitive help screens,* which automatically give the correct help screen for the process or feature you are using.

contiguous designates consecutive storage locations either in main memory or auxiliary storage. For example, a *contiguous* file is one that is stored with all records located physically together in adjacent storage positions.

continuous data analog data.

continuous feed the movement of paper through a printer without a break. See also **fan-fold paper.**

control code one or more characters entered into a program or command to initate some type of action. For example, in word processing, control codes entered in the text may cause underlining, boldface, the change of the font or pitch, or other print enhancements. As a command it may stop or start the scrolling of the text on the screen. See also **toggle.**

control key a key on the computer keyboard used to enter control codes. The control key works much like the shift key in that it is held down as the required key is pressed.

control unit the part of the CPU that directs all computer operations.

conventional memory internal data storage up to 640 kilobytes on IBM-compatible systems that can be addressed directly and sequentially by MS-DOS. See also **expanded memory** and **extended memory.**

coprocessor a special processor designed to work with or assist the primary CPU. Coprocessors cannot stand alone but are normally intended to enhance a particular area such as mathematical calculations or graphics display.

copy-protected refers to software that has been recorded in such a way as to make it very difficult to duplicate.

correspondence mode a setting available on many dot-matrix printers that produces near letter quality or letter quality print. See also **draft mode.**

courseware the textbook-type documentation that accompanies many educational software packages such as CAI materials.

cpi abbreviation for **characters per inch,** a measure of print pitch.

cpl abbreviation for **characters per line,** which is sometimes used as the measure of the number of characters that can be placed on one line by a printer or on a monitor screen.

CP/M a disk operating system for microcomputers that was very widely used until a few years ago. A few models are still around that offer CP/M as standard or as an option. A great deal of public domain software is available for most CP/M based systems.

cps 1. abbreviation for **characters per second,** a measure of the speed of a character printer. 2. abbreviation for **cycles per second,** or hertz, a measure of frequency.

CPU abbreviation for **central processing unit,** the part of the computer that controls and performs all processing activities. It consists of the ALU, control unit, and main memory. See also **microprocessor.**

CPU-intensive an operation that involves mostly processing within the CPU with limited disk access required. These are usually faster than disk-intensive processes but may require more memory. See also **ramdisk.**

CPU time the duration required for processing by the CPU. See also **connect time.**

crash an uncontrolled shutdown of the system.

CRT abbreviation for **cathode ray tube,** the large tube, the face of which we see as the picture tube of a television or the screen of a monitor.

cursor a symbol that marks the current position on the CRT screen and moves as the position changes. It is most often a single underline or a block the size of one character. It sometimes blinks.

cursor control key a key that can change the position of the cursor. These keys are often grouped together in a cursor control keypad.

cursor control keypad a special group of keys on a keyboard that perform cursor movement functions. Aside from the usual up, down, right, and left, they may include text editing, moving through a file by screens or other blocks, and jumping to specified points on the screen or in the file. See also **numeric keypad.**

cylinder the collection of all tracks on a disk that have the same number.

D

D/A see **D to A conversion.**

daisy-wheel a common type of printwheel that has its character set at the ends of a series of spokes radiating from a central hub.

DASD abbreviation for **direct access storage device,** which is any unit that permits direct access of data. For microcomputers this is usually a disk.

data an item or value to be processed.

data bank basically the same as a data base except that it may also refer to a collection of data bases.

data base a collection of data on a specific topic or for a designated purpose and organized for retrieval.

data base management system see **DBMS.**

data cassette a high-quality tape cassette designed for the storage of data on a computer.

data communications see **telecommunications.**

data communications channel a link used in telecommunications. The most common data communications channel for personal computers is the telephone line, but others include microwaves and communications satellites.

data density a measure of the amount of items or values stored in a unit length. On a tape this is usually in bits per inch, and on a disk it is in either bits per inch, tracks per inch, or both.

data file   a collection of related records that contains values to be processed or information that has been processed. See also **program file.**

data transfer rate   a measure of the speed (in bits per second) at which values are transferred from one point to another, such as from a CPU to a printer or remote terminal.

DBMS   abbreviation for **data base management system,** a software package consisting of a set of programs that govern the organization of, access to, and the maintenance of a data base.

D connector   a D-shaped link used by some computers for attaching a mouse, joystick, or other device. D connectors may also be used for RGB monitor connections.

DDP   abbreviation for **distributed data processing.**

debug   to locate and remove the errors (bugs) from a computer program.

debugging tool   a utility program that may come with the operating system and with other software that assists in the debugging of special programs. See also **patch.**

decimal number system   the base 10 number system that employs the ten digits 0–9. Since this system is not convenient for the representation of digital data, the binary, octal, and hexadecimal systems are most frequently used with computers.

dedicated line   see **leased line.**

default   a value that is automatically assumed and assigned whenever no other value is entered.

degradation   the slowing down of a system under the load of processing. This is usually noticeable only on multiuser systems or microcomputers running software that permits multiprocessing.

demodulation   see **modem.**

descender   the part of a lowercase character that prints below the line such as in letters *g, p,* and *y.*

desktop computer   see **microcomputer.**

desktop publisher   an application software package that is oriented toward output design. These programs provide for special printing features that permit the user to create and publish professional-looking layouts.

development system   the part of a software package that is designed to permit the user to develop new programs or design new applications.

development tool   a program designed to assist in the creation or modification of programs. See also **editor.**

device indicator   a number, letter, or group of characters that designate a specific device for data transfer.

diagnostic   1. an error message. 2. a check for an error condition.

dial-up line   a regular connection established through the telephone system. See also **leased line.**

digital   characterized by the representation of data by a series of signals and the presence (on) or absence (off) of each. For example, the numbers on a digital clock are formed by a set of little bars that make the pattern for each digit depending on which bars are "on" or "off." See also **analog.**

digital computer   an electronic device designed to process data in digital format. These general-purpose machines are suitable for most applications and are by far the most common type. All personal computers are digital. See also **analog computer.**

digitize   to transfer to digital format.

digitizer   a type of scanner that converts an analog image (such as a picture) into a series of digital values.

DIP switches   little switches, usually in groups of eight, found on computers, printers, modems, boards, and other devices that are set to either "on" or "off" to establish certain protocols. This permits the circuit to be adjusted without the need for actual physical modifications.

direct access   a method of storing data that permits any record or other data items to be obtained without the need for obtaining all the preceding items. See also **sequential access.**

direct access storage device   see **DASD.**

direct file   a method of organizing a collection of records that permits immediate access of each record. Generally, records in a direct file are not stored in a group but are scattered all over the disk and located by means of a key. See also **ISAM** and **sequential file.**

directory   a listing of the files available on a disk or part of a disk.

directory track   the section of a disk that contains the list of files on that disk.

discrete data   digital data.

disk   a flat, circular, metal or plastic platter coated with a thin layer of magnetic material on which data may be recorded as a series of magnetic signals arranged in circular patterns called tracks. A disk may be a single, flexible, portable unit or it may consist of several individual units in a fixed system. See also **diskette** and **hard disk.**

disk cache   1. a program designed to speed up disk operations, especially when a series of processes is involved. 2. a portion of main memory set aside for use by a disk cache program.

disk cartridge   a removable hard storage unit of about 5 to 20 megabytes that offers the speed and capacity of a hard disk and the portability of a diskette.

disk controller board   unit of electronic components that governs input/output operations to a disk system.

diskette   a small, portable data storage unit that consists of a single, often flexible disk used as a magnetic storage medium. Data is recorded as magnetic signals arranged in a series of circular patterns. Diskettes are available in three sizes—8, 5¼, and 3½ inches—but the 8-inch diskette is not used with personal computers. Diskettes range in storage capacity from a few hundred kilobytes to nearly 1½ megabytes. See also **hard disk, floppy disk, minidisk,** and **microdisk.**

disk-intensive   a process that involves many disk transfers. These are usually slower but require less memory than CPU-intensive processes. See also **segmentation.**

disk pack   a unit made up of more than one disk, physically connected with a common center shaft.

documentation   written material that accompanies a software package or a computer system that offers explanations for such things as its setup and operation, uses, features, capabilities, and so forth.

DOS   acronym for **D**isk **O**perating **S**ystem, a set of programs that activates the computer and allows the user to perform computer functions.

dot addressable   refers to the ability of a dot-matrix device such as a printer to display a graphics image by individual control of each dot.

dot-matrix   indicates characters that are formed by a series of dots, so closely spaced that the characters appear to be solid. Such symbols may be formed from a variety of techniques ranging from small pins striking a ribbon onto paper to tiny jets of ink. The quality of such print varies from a very poor "computer look" to an excellent letter quality imitation. See also **fully formed character.**

dot pitch   indicates the spacing of dots as on a color monitor screen.

double density   a data density for floppy disks at about 48 tracks per inch for 5¼-inch diskettes.

double-sided   a term that means that data can be recorded on both sides of a diskette.

download   to transfer a copy of a file from a host computer to a smaller computer, usually a microcomputer. See also **upload.**

downloadable characters   characters (or a set of characters) that can be sent to a printer or other output device to replace or supplement those normally available for use.

downtime   the interval a system (or any part of it) is unavailable for use.

dpi   abbreviation for **dots per inch,** a common measure of the resolution of a graphics display.

draft mode   the normal printing mode for most dot-matrix printers. The print quality varies widely but usually looks like computer print. See also **correspondence mode.**

DRAM   (dee-ram) acronym for **D**ynamic **R**andom **A**ccess **M**emory. See **dynamic allocation.**

drive   a unit that writes data to or reads it from a storage medium such as a tape or disk.

driver   a program that controls some component of the system such as a monitor, disk drive, or printer.

DS/DD   see **double-sided** and **double density.**

DS/HD   see **double-sided** and **high density.**

D to A conversion   the change of data or signals from digital to analog format. See also **A to D conversion** and **modem.**

dumb terminal   an input/output device that has no self-contained processing capability. See also **intelligent terminal.**

dump   1. a permanent copy of part or all of memory. 2. to make a permanent copy of part or all of memory.

duplex   the ability to transfer data in two directions. If the signals can go both ways at the same time, it is called *full duplex;* if simultaneous transmission is not permitted, it is known as *half-duplex.* See also **simplex.**

dynamic allocation   the division of main memory or other system resources so that each process is assigned whatever portion is needed as the program is being run. See also **static allocation.**

E

EAROM   (ear-rom) acronym for **E**lectrically **A**lterable **R**ead-**O**nly **M**emory, a ROM chip that can be reprogrammed electrically and usually rather quickly without the necessity of removing it from the circuit. See also **PROM** and **EPROM.**

EBCDIC   (ebb-see-dick) acronym for **E**xtended **B**inary **C**oded **D**ecimal **I**nterchange **C**ode, an older 8-bit coding system developed and still sometimes used by IBM. See also **ASCII.**

edit   to create or make changes in a document.

edit key   a button on the keyboard that permits certain changes to be made without the need of an editor.

editor   a program that permits you to create or make changes in a document. A word processor is an advanced type of editor. See also **development tool, line editor,** and **full-screen editor.**

EDP abbreviation for **electronic data processing.**

EFT abbreviation for **electronic funds transfer,** a system commonly used by banks and other money handlers that involves the computer-controlled conveyance of money between accounts.

EGA card IBM's **Enhanced Graphics Adapter,** a newer color graphics board for its PCs. This system is intended to replace the monochrome Hercules, MDPA, and color CGA cards. It offers more colors at a higher resolution than the older CGA board. See also **VGA card.**

EIA abbreviation for **Electronic Industries Association,** an organization of electrical equipment manufacturers that establishes standards for components used in data communications.

8-bit processor a microprocessor that handles data in 8-bit blocks and is slower than the newer 16-bit and 32-bit machines. Few computers use this type processor anymore.

80-column card an expansion board that permits computers that display only 40-column screens to expand to the 80-column format.

electronic bulletin board a data base normally accessed over telephone lines that provides a source of information and often message exchange for users with common interests.

electronic file cabinet a system for organizing, storing, and retrieving records using automated means, as with a data base management system.

electronic funds transfer see **EFT.**

electronic mail a method of sending and receiving messages through a multiuser system, bulletin board, network, or other system.

electronic shopping a method of shopping through catalogs and making purchases using a remote access terminal.

electrostatic printer a nonimpact serial printer that produces dot-matrix characters by placing electric charges on a specially coated paper to which dry ink particles adhere.

EMS abbreviation for **expanded memory specification.**

emulator a software program that permits a computer to appear to be and/or function as a different type system.

end user the final person or business to make use of a product or service. This is generally the consumer.

EPROM (ee-prom) acronym for Erasable Programmable Read-Only Memory, a ROM chip that can be reprogrammed after being exposed to high-intensity ultraviolet light for several minutes. See also **PROM** and **EAROM.**

ergonomic designed with the needs and comfort of the human user in mind.

even parity see **parity bit.**

executable file see **command file.**

expanded memory internal data storage beyond 640 kilobytes but less than 1 megabyte on IBM-compatible systems that is normally addressed by MS-DOS through paging. See also **conventional memory** and **extended memory.**

expanded memory specification a method used for addressing the expanded memory available in an IBM-compatible PC.

expansion board a unit of electronic components added to the capabilities of a computer. This may be additional memory or a new feature such as color graphics.

expansion slot a position for adding an expansion board.

export to transfer from the file format currently in use to another one. See also **import.**

extended memory internal data storage on IBM-compatible systems beyond 1 megabyte. See also **conventional memory** and **expanded memory.**

external storage see **auxiliary storage.**

F

fan-fold paper sheets that are connected end to end by perforation and usually with holes along each side (sometimes detachable) for continuous pin or tractor feeding through a printer.

FAT acronym for **F**ile **A**llocation **T**able, the part of the operating system on an MS-DOS disk that keeps track of the locations of all the files in the directory(ies) and allocates the remaining disk space to new files.

fatal error the cause of premature termination of processing, often as a crash.

father file see **grandfather system.**

F connector a type of video connector used by some computers.

fiber optics cable that is made of a series of very thin, flexible glass or plastic fibers through which data is transmitted using a light beam. Such cables have a very high data capacity.

field an individual item of data. For example, a name can be one field or three: first, middle, and last.

FIFO (fie-foe) acronym for **F**irst **I**n, **F**irst **O**ut, a process in which the first job put in line to be done is the first one to be processed. The line at the window of a movie theater is an example of a FIFO process. See also **LIFO** and **queue.**

file   a collection of related records. Data is normally stored as files. See also **data file** and **program file.**

file allocation table   see **FAT.**

file extension   an identifier of the type or purpose of a file, usually written as one to three letters following the filename and separated from it by a period. For example, the file PHONE.BAS might be a program written in BASIC while NUMBER.DAT could be a data file.

filename   the identification of a collection of related records in a storage system. Filenames must be unique and normally may contain up to eight characters but sometimes more. For example, a file that contains a list of telephone numbers might be called PHONE or TELNUM.

file specification   the complete description of a collection of related records, giving the filename, extension, and device indicator, if needed. For example, the file B:TELNUM.COM might be a command file named TELNUM and located on disk B. (Hard disk systems may also require directory or account specifications as well.)

file type   see **file extension.**

firmware   programs permanently stored on a ROM chip.

fixed disk   a nonremovable unit on which data is recorded. See also **disk.**

flexible disk   see **floppy disk.**

floppy disk   technically an 8- or 5¼-inch diskette, but the term is usually used interchangeably with **diskette.**

font   a print typeface (such as Roman, Courier, and Orator) or style (such as block and script).

footer   a special message or identification placed at the bottom of a page.

footprint   the space on a floor or table occupied by a piece of hardware.

format   1. to initialize. 2. to form into a specific pattern. 3. a specific pattern.

FORTRAN   acronym for **FOR**mula **TRAN**slation, a high-level programming language designed to be used primarily for mathematical, scientific, and engineering applications. FORTRAN was the first high-level language to be developed successfully; it was introduced by IBM in 1957.

frame   1. see **page frame.** 2. a block of bits transmitted as a single unit.

freeware   software that is freely distributed without charge (other than a small service fee) to all interested users. See also **public domain software** and **shareware.**

friction feed   a method of moving paper continuously through a printer by using only the friction between the paper and the platen. This method is employed when single sheets are used. See also **pin feed, sheet feeder,** and **tractor feed.**

full duplex   see **duplex.**

full-screen editor   a program that permits changes to be performed at any point on the screen by simply moving the cursor to the appropriate position and making the change. See also **line editor.**

full-stroke key   the type found on most keyboards characterized by a marked give or depression when pressed, often with an associated key-click. These keys are most like those on an electric typewriter and are preferred by most users. See also **limited-stroke key** and **touch-sensitive keyboard.**

fully formed character   a letter or symbol that is formed by a solid, unbroken image, as with a printwheel. See also **dot-matrix.**

function key   a key that can be programmed to perform a specific operation. This may be a permanent programming by the operating system or temporary programming by the user or the application software in use.

G

GB   abbreviation for **gigabyte.**

giga-   a prefix meaning one billion.

gigabyte   one billion bytes.

GIGO   (gig-go) acronym for **G**arbage-**I**n, **G**arbage-**O**ut. This is a colorful way of saying that the output cannot be reliable if the input is not.

glitch   a nonreproducible problem in a system. Glitches often result from voltage fluctuations, static discharges, and data transmission errors. See also **soft error.**

grandfather file   see **grandfather system.**

grandfather system   a method of storing data for making backups that makes use of three rotating copies. The most recent copy is called the *son file,* the middle one is the *father file,* and the oldest is referred to as the *grandfather file.*

graphics   the capability to produce special characters or drawings such as graphs, charts, and picturelike representations of various objects.

graphics board   an expansion device that adds the memory and software necessary to give a system graphics capability.

graphics printer   a printer that is capable of producing hard copy of graphics outputs, usually by forming images from a pattern of individual dots. See also **dot addressable.**

graphics tablet   see **tablet.**

H

H a suffix that, when used at the end of a number (such as 384H), indicates the hexadecimal format has been used in expressing that number. See also **hexadecimal number system.**

hacker 1. a nonprofessional computer whiz. 2. one who tries to gain unlawful access to a computer system.

half-duplex see **duplex.**

half-height drive a disk drive that is half the physical height of older models without sacrificing storage capacity.

handshaking the communication between computers or a computer and its peripherals in which control codes are exchanged to govern the transfer of data.

hardcard a hard disk mounted directly on a card.

hard character any letter or symbol entered into a text by the user. They may be moved but are normally unchanged otherwise. See also **soft character.**

hard copy a reproduction that is exhibited on a permanent medium and is in user-readable format, such as a printed page. See also **soft copy.**

hard disk a magnetic data storage system composed of one or more rigid platters. Data is recorded as magnetic signals arranged in a pattern of concentric circles on the surfaces. Storage capacities range from about 10 megabytes up to several hundred megabytes. See also **diskettes.**

hard error a permanent problem that is not removed by rereading the data or any other action. This usually means that there is a flaw such as a bad spot on a disk that must be avoided in the future. See also **glitch** and **soft error.**

hard-sectored description of a floppy disk on which holes are used to mark the positions of the individual sectors on the tracks rather than special records. See also **soft-sectored.**

hardware the physical equipment of a computer system, such as the computer, monitor, and printer.

hardware selectable a feature of some devices that permits certain of its options to be selected by switches, buttons, or dials on the unit. For example, you might be able to change the print pitch or font from a control panel on the printer. See also **software selectable.**

hard-wired 1. connected to the CPU with a cable. 2. permanently wired.

hash total the sum obtained from adding the digits in a field. This value is then checked with a sum calculated at an earlier time to check for possible data errors.

Hayes-compatible a modem (or sometimes telecommunications software) that uses and recognizes the commands and protocols of the Hayes modem systems, which have become the unofficial standards in this area.

head the part of a drive that writes data to the storage medium (disk or tape) or reads data from it.

head crash a condition that results from the read/write head of a hard disk drive coming in contact with the disk surface. This usually causes permanent damage to the disk surface at the point of contact.

header 1. a special message or identification placed at the top of a page. 2. an identifying marker or value in a record, file, or data transfer string.

Hercules card a non-IBM-produced monochrome graphics system for IBM-compatibles that is supported by many software packages, making it an unofficial industry standard. See also **CGA card, EGA card, MDPA card,** and **VGA card.**

hertz a measure of frequency or the number of cycles in a given time expressed in cycles per second (cps).

heuristic developed by a trial-and-error approach using evaluations of prior results. See also **modular program** and **structured programming.**

hex indicates that numbers are represented according to the hexadecimal number system. It is sometimes written as a subscript such as 384_{hex}.

hexadecimal number system a number system based on the number 16 and using the sixteen characters 0–9 and A–F. Since a group of four binary digits can be expressed as one hexadecimal digit, this system is often used to express binary values in a more compact format. For example, 100111000011 (binary) = 9C3 (hex). Hexadecimal numbers may be indicated in several ways, including 9C3H, $9C3_{hex}$, and $9C3_{16}$. See also **binary number system** and **octal number system.**

hierarchy the arrangement of hardware, software, and processing according to some specific set of priorities.

high density a storage system that permits 1.2 and 1.44 megabytes on a single 5¼- and 3½-inch diskette, respectively. See also **quad density.**

high-level language a programming language such as BASIC and COBOL that is designed to be portable and user-friendly.

high-resolution showing great detail; the higher the resolution of a graphics monitor or printer, the greater the detail of a drawing or image it is able to reproduce.

host computer a computer that serves as a source for data and information retrieval for other computers, usually microcomputers.

hub ring the rigid center hole of a floppy disk; it is intended to prevent the drive mechanism from damaging the disk as it spins.

I

IBM-compatible a computer that can run software written for an IBM computer.

IC abbreviation for **integrated circuit,** an assembly of electrical components deposited and connected on a silicon wafer. See also **board** and **printed circuit board.**

icon a graphics image, normally used to represent a specific thing or to cause a desired action to occur.

IEEE abbreviation for **Institute of Electrical and Electronics Engineers,** an organization of electrical engineering professionals established to promote the advancement, propagation, and excellence of electrical, electronic, and computer technology.

impact printer one that produces characters on the paper by actually striking the paper through the ribbon, much like a typewriter. Examples include dot-matrix printers, with printheads using arrays of pins or wires, and models that use a printwheel. See also **nonimpact printer.**

import to transfer from another file format into the one currently in use. See also **export.**

index a list of the keys and associated addresses for each record in a file.

indexed sequential file see **ISAM.**

index file the list of record keys and addresses that is part of an ISAM file.

index hole position indicators at the beginning of a track in a diskette for *soft-sectored* disks and each sector for *hard-sectored* disks.

information values that are the result of processing data.

initialize to set up or prepare; to *initialize a disk* is to make it ready for use by a system.

initial program load see **IPL.**

ink-jet printer a serial printer that uses tiny jets of charged ink particles to form dot-matrix-type characters, usually of good quality.

input tablet see **tablet.**

insert mode an editing method offered by many software packages that permits characters to be inserted in between others. See also **overwrite mode.**

instruction a command to the CPU to carry out an operation.

integrated circuit see **IC.**

integrated software a programming package that offers two or more types of applications, such as a word processor, spreadsheet, or data base manager.

intelligent terminal an input/output device that has independent computing power. When a microcomputer ties into another using a data communications channel, it is acting as an intelligent terminal. See also **dumb terminal.**

interactive processing a method whereby immediate feedback is received when programs or data are entered into the system. Most microcomputers use this mode. See also **batch processing.**

interface 1. the boundary or connection between two components such as the CPU and a printer. 2. to connect two components together.

interleave to alternate as in program instructions or the selection of data from more than one source.

internal storage see **main memory.**

interpreter a program that translates a source program written in a high-level language into an object program in machine language, line by line, executing each line as it is converted. The process is repeated until the end of the program or an error condition is found. Error messages are usually provided as problems are encountered. See also **assembler** and **compiler.**

interrupt 1. a temporary halt to the execution of a program during which the operating system tranfers control to another process. 2. to cause an interrupt.

I/O abbreviation for **input/output.**

I/O controller board a unit with various electronic components that controls and directs the signals between the CPU and the various input/output devices.

IPL abbreviation for **initial program load,** essentially the same as boot but the term is more often used for larger systems.

ips abbreviation for **inches per second,** a measurement of the speed at which a tape drive moves the tape across the read/write heads.

ISAM (eye-sam) acronym for Indexed Sequential Access Method, a procedure for locating files using an index that gives a key and the address of each individual record. Although ISAM files are stored sequentially and can be accessed that way, direct access is also possible by means of the index file. See also **direct file** and **sequential file.**

iterative repetitive.

J

JCL abbreviation for **job control language.** This is a set of instructions used to control operations through the operating system. Traditionally, JCLs have not been very complex for microcomputers, but with the more powerful models now becoming available, JCLs are likely to be more important. Most personal computers have user-friendly programs to interface with the JCL and make it easy to use.

job accounting system   a program that maintains a record of all the processes run by the computer. This may provide such information as what was done, who did it, from where it was done, and how long it took. Such programs are very useful when users are to be billed for their computer usage.

job control language   see **JCL.**

joystick   a device for manually controlling the cursor, an object on the screen, or other screen action by the movement of a stick back and forth, right and left, or by the push of a button. Joysticks are used with games and other programs that have graphics.

justification   spacing text so that the right-hand margin is even and blocked like the left-hand margin.

K

K   abbreviation for **k**ilobyte, which is exactly 1,024 bytes but is usually rounded off to 1,000 bytes.

KB   another abbreviation for **kilobyte.**

key   1. a data item, usually a field within a record, used to identify the record uniquely. 2. a button on a keyboard.

keyboard   an arrangement of buttons in a typewriterlike layout that is used to enter, copy, move, and otherwise manipulate data manually and enter instructions to direct the computer's operations.

keyclick   an audible sound emitted by many keyboards whenever a key is depressed.

keypad   a set of keys grouped together and performing a particular function.

kilo-   a prefix meaning 1,000.

kilobyte   1,000 bytes.

L

LAN   acronym for **L**ocal **A**rea **N**etwork, a system of two or more PCs within a localized area (such as a building) that share some of the same facilities, such as disk, printers, and software. See also **bus network, ring network,** and **star network.**

laptop   a class of portable, briefcase-sized computers. Some laptops function as little more than remote terminals, while others are complete systems offering powerful and advanced features and capabilities.

laser printer   an expensive, fast, versatile page printer that produces very high quality print and graphics.

LCD   abbreviation for **liquid crystal display,** the dark-on-light display seen on most calculators and digital watches. LCD screens are used on many laptop computers, but they are difficult to see in poor light. This has caused some resistance to their use, but improved technology in this area should soon change this. See also **LED.**

leased line   a private, permanent connection that permits continuous access, usually at a fixed rate. See also **dial-up line.**

LED   abbreviation for **light-emitting diode,** a small electrical component that gives out light when a current is passed through it. LEDs are set in patterns to form numbers or other symbols when certain diodes are illuminated. They are commonly used on calculator and clock displays. See also **LCD.**

letter quality   see **LQ.**

library   a collection of programs, routines, or subroutines available to a program or user.

license agreement   see **software license agreement.**

LIFO   (lie-foe) acronym for **L**ast **I**n, **F**irst **O**ut, a process in which the first job in line to be done is the last one to be processed. Placing papers in a pile and then removing them one by one from the top is an example of a LIFO process. See also **FIFO** and **stack.**

light pen   an input device that consists of a stylus on the end of a cable connected to the monitor. It can sense the light from a particular position on the screen and can be used to create, delete, or move images on the screen.

LIM   acronym for **L**otus/**I**ntel/**M**icrosoft, a standard for addressing extended memory in IBM-compatibles in excess of 1 megabyte.

limited-stroke key   the type of key found on some keyboards and most calculators that depresses only slightly when pressed. Those who do a lot of typing on their systems usually find them unsatisfactory. See also **full-stroke key** and **touch-sensitive keyboard.**

linear memory   memory that can be addressed continuously, as opposed to being addressed through paging.

line editor   a program that permits changes to be performed only on one line at a time. See also **full-screen editor.**

line printer   a device that prints one entire line at a time. See also **character printer** and **page printer.**

linkage editor a system utility program that combines one or more object programs and any necessary library routines into a single loadable object file by establishing all required links for data transfer between the involved files.

linking loader a linkage editor that performs the functions of a loader.

list an ordered sequence. See also **queue** and **stack.**

load to bring into memory. See also **retrieve, save,** and **store.**

loader a system utility program that brings (loads) an object program from an auxiliary storage unit into main memory.

local area network see **LAN.**

logical drive a section of a physical drive that has been set aside and designated as an independent storage device. For example, a physical drive of 70 megabytes might be divided into logical drives of 20, 20, and 30 megabytes. See also **partition.**

logical operation a comparison between two items to determine a relationship, such as whether one number is larger than another or whether one name comes before another in a list.

lpi abbreviation for **lines per inch,** a measure of the number of lines a printer prints per inch, usually either six or eight.

lpm abbreviation for **lines per minute,** a measure of the speed of a line printer.

LQ abbreviation for **letter quality,** which indicates that the characters are of the same high quality as those from a good electric typewriter. Printers that use printwheels, some dot-matrix printers, and the more costly ink-jet and laser systems have the capability to produce letter quality characters.

LSI abbreviation for **large-scale integration,** refers to circuits first developed in the early 1970s that permitted tens of thousands of transistors and other electrical components to be placed on a single board.

luma the intensity part of a video signal. See also **chroma** and **separated composite.**

M

Mac short for *Apple Macintosh* computer.

machine language programming instructions expressed in binary format or in the basic coding of the computer. Such programs are very difficult to write, are not portable, but are very fast and can be run directly without any need of a translator.

machine-readable format   any format that can be read directly by the computer such as a disk or tape. See also **user-readable format.**

machine-specific   software that can be run on only one type or model of computer.

Macintosh   a general-purpose Apple computer that employs a mouse and icon-based operating system to make it user-friendly.

macro command   a series of instructions that can be initiated by a single short command.

magnetic disk   see **disk.**

magnetic tape   see **tape.**

mainframe   a large computer capable of handling many users and running many programs simultaneously. Such systems are fast and support a wide range of peripherals. They are normally found in large businesses, universities, and government agencies.

main memory   the set of data storage locations found inside the computer and directly accessible by the CPU. Memories can vary from a few dozen kilobytes to several megabytes. See also **auxiliary storage.**

mark-sense reader   see **OMR.**

matrix   an array or an ordered arrangement. For example, 63 dots might be arranged into a rectangular matrix or array of nine rows and seven columns.

MB   abbreviation for **megabyte.**

MDPA card   IBM's **Monochrome Display and Printer Adapter,** an older monochrome graphics card for its PCs. See also **CGA card, EGA card, Hercules card,** and **VGA card.**

meg   short for **megabyte.**

mega-   a prefix meaning 1 million.

megabyte   1 million bytes.

megahertz   1 million hertz.

memory   see **main memory.**

memory-resident   see **resident.**

menu   a list of available options; a *Menu of System Commands* might show all the system utilities that can be used on that system. See also **shell.**

menu-driven   a program or system that uses a series of menus to make it more user-friendly. The user may select the desired option by either typing the corresponding letter or number or moving the cursor to the proper selection and hitting the Return or Enter key, and the program will then automatically call up the proper routines. When the desired processing is done, the menu returns to the screen for other options. Some systems use several layers of menus.

merge   to combine. A typical example would be to merge a name and address file with a form letter.

MICR   abbreviation for **magnetic ink character recognition,** a system that reads characters which have been printed in a magnetic ink. This system is most frequently used by banks and similar financial institutions.

micro-   a prefix meaning one millionth.

micro   1. a shorthand term for microcomputer. 2. very small.

microchip   a very tiny chip.

microcomputer   a small computer that uses a *microprocessor* for a CPU and has limited input/output capabilities.

microdisk   a 3½-inch diskette.

microjustification   the even spacing between words on each line of a text that has a blocked right margin.

micron   one millionth of a meter or one thousandth of a millimeter.

microprocessor   the CPU of a microcomputer. Microprocessors have an ALU and control unit with limited memory such as a scratchpad. The main memory is usually added separately.

microsecond   one millionth of a second.

milli-   a prefix meaning one thousandth.

millisecond   one thousandth of a second.

minicomputer   a medium-sized computer capable of handling several users and multiprogramming, and normally found in small businesses and colleges.

minidisk   a 5¼-inch diskette.

Minimal BASIC   an ANSI standard BASIC of only limited capability but recommended by ANSI to be included as part of all versions of that language.

MHz   abbreviation for **megahertz.**

mnemonic   a memory aid.

mnemonic code   a symbol or set of characters used as a mnemonic.

mode   a condition or set of conditions for operation, as a printer may have modes for different print qualities.

modem   (moe-dem) acronym for **MO**dulator/**DEM**odulator, a device used to connect digital devices to analog data communications channels. Modems perform the D to A *(modulation)* and A to D *(demodulation)* conversions necessary to translate the data from the digital format used by the computer system to the analog version required for the transfer of data over such channels as telephone lines, microwaves, and satellites.

modular program   a program constructed from and consisting of interacting modules. The individual modules are often developed independently and normally form self-contained units that are then combined to form the completed program. See also **structured programming.**

modulation   see **modem.**

module   1. a section of a program that performs one or more specific functions. 2. a plug-in component.

monitor   a device having a CRT screen used for visual display with a computer. Monitors are similar to TVs but do not have a tuner and cannot receive ordinary television broadcast signals. Since they do not have to send the signal through the tuner circuits, a sharper image is usually obtained. See also **receiver.**

monitor/receiver   a television receiver that is also designed to act as a monitor. Such a device can display a video signal without sending it through the tuner, thus producing a sharper image.

monochrome   one color.

motherboard   1. a board onto which other boards are mounted. 2. the main board.

mouse   a device for manually controlling the cursor, an object on the screen, or other screen action by the movement of a palm-sized device on a flat surface. A small ball on the bottom of the mouse rolls with the direction of the motion, transferring this action to the screen. One or two buttons are also used for additional control, such as capture and release. A mouse is used extensively by the *Apple Macintosh* and many graphics packages on other systems.

MP/M   a multiuser version of CP/M.

ms   abbreviation for **millisecond.**

μs   abbreviation for **microsecond.**

MS-DOS   the version of the IBM PC-DOS disk operating system used by IBM-compatible computers.

MTBF   abbreviation for **mean time between failures,** an expression of the reliability of a piece of equipment that gives the average time that the component will function before a failure occurs. MTBF values may apply to the entire component or only to a specific part, such as to the printhead of a printer.

MTTR   abbreviation for **mean time to repair,** an expression of a manufacturer's claim as to the average time to repair a certain piece of equipment. Such values normally reflect only the actual bench or work time and not delays from processing or a backlog, which can be much longer.

multiplexor   a device that permits more than one terminal to share the same input/output port. Although each device has direct access to the

CPU and system, the data transfer rate is reduced by the number of devices that are connected.

multiprocessing the ability to perform more than one process at the same time by using more than one processor.

multiprogramming see **multitasking.**

multi-sync designates a monitor that employs variable frequencies to achieve a higher resolution.

multitasking the ability to run more than one program at the same time. Since one processor is being shared by all of the programs, the run-times may be significantly increased. Although provided by some software, it is often not very practical or efficient on personal computers. See also **time-sharing.**

multiuser designed to support more than one user at a time. Although most microcomputers are single-user machines, a few powerful systems have multiuser capability. See also **multiprocessing** and **multitasking.**

N

nano- a prefix meaning one billionth.

nanosecond one billionth of a second.

network any system of two or more computers along with all the connected peripherals organized to share resources. See also **bus network, LAN, ring network,** and **star network.**

NLQ abbreviation for **near letter quality,** which indicates characters that are close to the quality of those from a good electric typewriter. Many dot-matrix printers now offer this mode as a standard feature.

node a point in a network.

noise 1. unwanted signals. 2. interference.

noise filter an electric device designed to eliminate noise.

nonimpact printer a device that produces print without physically striking the paper. Examples include ink-jet, thermal, electrostatic, and laser printers. See also **impact printer.**

nonvolatile a main memory or auxiliary storage design in which the stored data is not lost when the power is removed from the system. See also **volatile.**

ns abbreviation for **nanosecond.**

numeric containing only numbers, which may include only the ten digits 0–9, a plus or minus sign, and a decimal point.

numeric keypad a group of keys set aside for the entry of numeric data and performing simple arithmetic operations. See also **cursor control keypad.**

nybble   half a **byte.**

O

object program   the machine-language version of a source program that is produced by an assembler or compiler.

OCR   abbreviation for **optical character reader,** an input device that can read printed material provided it is printed in a font and pitch the reader is programmed to recognize. See also **OMR** and **scanner.**

octal   indicates that numbers are represented according to the octal number system.

octal number system   a number system based on the number 8 and using the eight digits 0–7. Since a group of three binary digits can be expressed as one octal digit, this system is often used to express binary values in a more compact format. For example, 100111000011 (binary) = 4703 (octal). A subscript of 8 such as 4703_8 is sometimes used to indicate an octal number. See also **binary number system** and **hexadecimal number system.**

odd parity   see **parity bit.**

OEM   abbreviation for **original equipment manufacturer.**

offline   not connected to the CPU either physically or electronically.

OMR   abbreviation for **optical mark reader,** a device designed to detect the presence or absence of marks from a predetermined pattern on a page. See also **OCR** and **scanner.**

online   connected to the CPU for ready access.

operating system   see **OS.**

operation   an action taken by a computer in response to an instruction.

optical character reader   see **OCR.**

optical mark reader   see **OMR.**

optical scanner   see **scanner.**

original equipment manufacturer   the company that is responsible for the initial construction of a product.

OS   abbreviation for **operating system,** the set of software programs that are necessary to control the basic operation of the computer.

OS/2   a new operating system for advanced IBM compatibles that makes use of multitasking.

overlay   1. a segment of a program that is loaded into main memory as needed and then overwritten by other overlays. This technique is used when the overall program is too large for it to fit in memory at one time. See also **segmentation** and **virtual memory.** 2. a guide supplied with some software that fits over a set of keys on a keyboard to show their assigned function.

overstrike   the situation when two or more characters are printed or displayed at the same position.

overwrite mode   an editing method offered by many software packages that causes characters to print over and replace the ones already on the screen at the cursor position. See also **insert mode.**

P

page   a section of a program of fixed length.

page frame   a block of main memory for storing one page.

page printer   a high-speed nonimpact device that prints an entire page at one time. Laser printers are page printers. See also **character printers** and **line printers.**

paging   1. the division of main memory into page frames. 2. the ability of an editor or word processor to divide a document by pages automatically.

paint   to draw directly on the CRT screen, such as with a light pen.

palette   the selection of colors or shades available with a graphics package.

parallel port   a type of connection that transmits data one byte at a time. Parellel ports are most frequently used for printers on IBM-compatible systems. See also **Centronics port** and **serial port.**

parity bit   an extra bit added to a storage location and used for error checking. This is done by counting the number of bits that are "on" to determine if the sum is odd *(odd parity)* or even *(even parity)*. The result should correspond with earlier counts.

partition   1. the division of main memory into parts to be used in a multiprogramming system. See also **dynamic allocation** and **static allocation.** 2. the division of a physical drive into two or more logical drives. For example, a 40-megabyte hard disk might be *partitioned* into two 20-megabyte disks. Such a drive will then behave as though it were two 20-megabyte disks rather than a single 40-megabyte unit.

Pascal   a general-purpose, high-level programming language suitable for the beginner. It is considered to be a good language for learning good programming techniques because it is designed for structured programming.

password   a series of characters used as an identifying code to permit access to a system or file.

patch   1. a change made in an existing machine-language program. 2. to make a change in a machine-language program. See also **debugging tool.**

PC   1. abbreviation for **personal computer.** 2. sometimes used to denote an IBM personal computer.

PC-compatible   sometimes used to mean IBM PC-compatible.

PC-DOS   the disk operating system for IBM microcomputers.

peripheral   an attachment to a computer such as a modem or printer.

persistence   the length of time that a monitor holds an image on the screen.

personal computer   a small microcomputer designed to be both user-friendly and available at relatively low cost. Such systems offer software for applications that are of interest in everyday life. See also **PC.**

physical drive   the entire disk consisting of all logical drives into which that drive has been partitioned. For example, if a 60-megabyte disk is partitioned into two 30-megabyte logical drives, then the 60 megabytes represents the physical drive.

pico-   a prefix meaning one trillionth.

picosecond   one trillionth of a second.

pin feed   a method of moving paper through a printer by fitting pins at each end of the platen into holes on the sides of the paper. This method is used for continuous feed, but if a large throughput or different-width paper is needed, a tractor feed is recommended. See also **friction feed, sheet feeder,** and **tractor feed.**

pipeline   the direct transfer of data from one program to another without the need of any input/output operations. See also **shell** and **UNIX.**

pitch   a print size, such as pica (10 characters per inch) and elite (12 characters per inch).

pixel   the smallest point that can be addressed on a CRT screen.

platen   the device (usually a cylinder) that supports the paper in a printer.

platter   a single hard disk.

plotter   a device designed to produce a hard copy of graphics output by means of solid lines and curves.

plug-compatible   units from different manufacturers that can be plugged together and will communicate and work properly.

pointer   a marker as to a place in memory or in a file.

port   a position on a computer to connect a peripheral such as a printer or modem. See also **serial port, parallel port,** and **slot.**

portability 1. the ability of a program to be executed on different-type computers. 2. the ease of carrying a system from one place to another.

portable see **laptop.**

power conditioner an electrical device designed to eliminate both **voltage spikes** and **noise** from input power sources.

power director similar to a power strip except that each outlet is provided with an individual on/off switch.

power strip an electrical device, usually having an on/off switch and a circuit breaker, that provides multiple outlets.

ppm abbreviation for **pages per minute,** a measure of the speed of a page printer.

primary memory see **main memory.**

printed circuit board a thin laminated board with the circuit connections imprinted and the circuit elements fitted into sockets. See also **board** and **integrated circuit.**

printer a device designed to produce hard copy output, usually of text materials but possibly other items such as graphics images.

printer/plotter a device that serves the functions of either a printer or a plotter.

printhead the part of a serial, dot-matrix printer that produces the pattern for each character.

print spooler a software program that produces a list of files to be printed and sends these to the printer as soon as it is available, thus freeing the system for other uses.

printwheel a device used on an impact, letter quality printer to produce a given print font. These are similar in function to the typing elements found on many typewriters. See also **daisy-wheel** and **thimble.**

procedure-oriented describes a program or system that is designed to expedite the processes or procedures needed to complete a job or application. For example, a job control language is procedure-oriented. See also **application software, system software,** and **user-oriented.**

processor see **CPU** and **microprocessor.**

program 1. a logical sequence of instructions designed to accomplish a specific task. 2. to construct a program.

program file a collection of records that contains one or more instructions. Program files may also be data files if they serve as the input or output for other programs. Examples of this are the source and object programs for a compiler.

programmable key see **function key.**

programmer one who writes programs.

PROM acronym for **P**rogrammable **R**ead-**O**nly **M**emory, a type of ROM chip that is programmed by the manufacturer to suit the customer's individual needs. See also **EAROM** and **EPROM.**

prompt a character, symbol, sound, or message sent to the screen to signal the user that the computer is ready for input.

proportional spacing the characteristic of some print fonts where narrow characters such as *I* and *l* use less space than wider ones such as *H* and *M.*

proprietary 1. patented or copyrighted. 2. exclusively owned by a company or individual.

protocol a set of signals that must be transmitted and properly received before any data is sent in order to ensure that all parts of the system can communicate properly.

ps abbreviation for **picosecond.**

PS abbreviation for **proportional spacing.**

PS/2 a newer and more advanced (and expensive) IBM PC.

public domain software programs that are not owned or copyrighted by anyone and are available to all who want them without restriction. These programs can usually be obtained for a small service fee. See also **freeware** and **shareware.**

Q

quad density a high data density for floppy disks at about 96 tracks per inch on 5¼-inch diskettes. See also **high density.**

query language a high-level language that provides access to the information in a data base by requesting responses to specific questions (queries).

queue an ordered list in which values are inserted at one end and removed from the other. Data in a queue is usually handled as a *FIFO process* in which the first to be added to the list is the first to be processed. See also **stack.**

R

RAM acronym for **R**andom **A**ccess **M**emory, a read/write type of memory that permits the user to both read the information that is there and write data to it. This is the type of memory available to the user in most systems. See also **ROM.**

ramdisk the storage of files in main memory on a simulated disk drive to take advantage of the much higher processing speed of RAM. Such files can be recalled from or saved to the ramdisk area the same as with a regular disk but much faster. Ramdisk files must be saved to the disk for permanent storage. See also **CPU-intensive** and **disk-intensive.**

random access   see **direct access.**

random file   see **direct file.**

RCA connector   a type of link normally used to connect audio components that is used for composite video input to the monitor on some computer systems.

receiver   refers to an ordinary television when used as a visual display device. See also **monitor.**

record   a collection of related fields or data items.

register   a memory location within the ALU or control unit that is used for the temporary storage of instructions or data as they are processed.

relative file   see **direct file.**

remote access   access to a computer through a data communications channel.

resident   permanently present as a program that is *resident in memory* remains in memory at all times.

resolution   indicates the degree of detail that can be perceived.

response time   the interval between the input of a request or a command and the return of the required response.

retrieve   to obtain data from main memory or auxiliary storage. See also **load, save,** and **store.**

reverse video   displaying dark characters on a light background.

RF modulator   a transmitter, usually in the UHF television band, that permits an ordinary TV to be used as a monitor.

ring network   a design in which several computers are connected together in a circular pattern. Each computer may support its own set of peripherals and share the resources of some or all of the rest of the computers in the network. See also **bus network** and **star network.**

RGB video   short for **Red/Green/Blue video,** a video input method with separate inputs that provides improved color mixing and sharpness and is capable of producing relatively high resolution graphics displays. See also **composite video.**

R/O   abbreviation for **read-only.** See also **write-protected.**

R/O file   a collection of related records that can be read but not changed.

ROM   acronym for **R**ead-**O**nly **M**emory, a type of storage that permits its reading and use but not any changes. ROMs are preprogrammed at the factory for a specific purpose and are found on many boards such as graphics and in many systems that automatically boot when turned on. See also **RAM** and **PROM.**

rotational delay   the time required for the desired record on a disk to spin into position under the read/write head. See also **access time** and **seek time.**

routine   a set of instructions to solve a specific problem.

RS-232-C port   a standard 25-pin serial connection used by most microcomputers. It is most frequently used for a mouse, modem, speech synthesizer, or similar device. This 25-pin system is now an industry standard for data communications.

run   1. to execute a program. 2. the execution of a program.

run-time   the amount of time required for a program to run.

run-time system   the part of a software package that permits programs to be run.

R/W   abbreviation for **read/write.**

R/W file   a file that can be both read and written to (changed).

R/W head   see **head.**

S

save   to make a permanent copy of data in main memory on an auxiliary storage device. See also **load, retrieve,** and **store.**

scanner   an input device that is designed to recognize patterns of printed or drawn markings ranging from simple, fine, detailed lines to pages from a book to complex graphics symbols. See also **OCR** and **OMR.**

scratchpad memory   a small high-speed memory used by the CPU for the temporary storage of instructions or data.

scrolling   the ability to move the lines of print on a CRT screen up or down.

secondary storage   see **auxiliary storage.**

sector   a section of a track on a disk.

seek time   the time required for the access arm of a disk drive to move the read/write heads to the proper track or cylinder. See also **access time** and **rotational delay.**

segmentation   the division of large programs into portions that are loaded into main memory as needed, overwriting those that are no longer required. This permits programs to be run that are larger than the available memory. See also **overlay** and **virtual memory.**

separated composite   a video input method that separates the color *(chroma)* and intensity *(luma)*, recombining them on the screen.

sequential access   a method of storing data in which all records and other data items are read in order. See also **direct access.**

sequential file   a method of organizing a collection of records in which it is necessary to process each record in the same order that it was stored. See also **direct file** and **ISAM.**

serial access   see **sequential access.**

serial port   a type of connection that transmits data one bit at a time. Serial ports are commonly used by most input/output devices. See also **RS-232-C port** and **parallel port.**

serial printer   see **character printer.**

shareware   user-supported software that is copyrighted for which the author(s) usually request a small ($5 to $25) donation from those who use the program and find it of value. See also **public domain software.**

sheet feeder   a device that attaches to some printers that automatically and continuously moves single sheets through the printer, thus eliminating the need to use fan-fold or hand-feed the pages. See also **friction feed, pin feed,** and **tractor feed.**

shell   an on-screen menu found with some types of operating systems that permits system control through selecting various menu options. Shells tend to be interactive with their system, even initiating the transfer of data from one program to another. See also **pipeline** and **UNIX.**

shift key   a key that changes the function of a character printed by another key when pressed along with that key.

simplex   the ability to transfer data in only one direction at a time. See also **duplex.**

single-density   a low data density for floppy disks used only on 8-inch diskettes.

single-sided   a diskette that can record data on only one side.

single-user   designed to support only one user at any one time. By definition, personal computers are single-user systems.

16-bit processor   a microprocessor that handles data in 16-bit blocks. Most PCs are now of this or the faster 32-bit design and are faster than the older 8-bit machines.

slot   similar to a port but usually used for internal expansions such as memory, graphics, and so forth, by the addition of boards.

soft character   a letter or symbol entered into a text by the software to perform some special function, such as in the formatting of paragraphs by a word processor. These include spaces, returns, and hyphens that are then automatically deleted if no longer required. See also **hard character.**

soft copy   a reproduction that is in user-readable format but is not on a permanent medium, such as a display on a CRT screen. See also **hard copy.**

soft error a temporary problem that can be removed by rereading the data or some other action. See also **glitch** and **hard error.**

soft-sectored a description of a floppy disk on which the sectors on each track are marked by records. Most microcomputers now use this method. See also **hard-sectored.**

software the programs that are run on a computer. See also **application software** and **system software.**

software license agreement a legal instrument accompanying most software packages that states the terms under which the company is providing its material to the consumer. It covers such things as permissible copies, if any; number of machines on which the programs may be run; whether it is a purchase or lease; and procedures for obtaining replacement copies and updates, and for reporting bugs.

software selectable the ability to select certain features of a component of the system directly from the software. For example, a word processor may permit you to use various print enhancements such as underline or boldface by entering control codes directly into the text. See also **hardware selectable.**

son file see **grandfather system.**

sort to arrange information in a specified order, such as alphabetical, numerical, or chronological.

sound baffle an enclosure that fits over a printer or other device that helps reduce the operating noise to an acceptable level.

sound synthesizer an output device that produces sounds ranging from musical notes to spoken words.

source program a set of instructions written in assembly or a high-level language that is translated and processed by an assembler, compiler, or interpreter. See also **object program.**

speech synthesizer an output device that simulates human speech.

spindle the central shaft of a hard disk.

split screen a method of dividing the CRT screen to show two or more operations at once, but it may be that more than one is not in action at the same time. See also **window.**

spreadsheet a software package designed for the development and representation of a variety of financial applications.

sprite graphics special characters or drawings that involve motion, usually of an object against a background that is either fixed or has a different motion.

SPSS abbreviation for **Statistical Package for the Social Sciences,** a comprehensive program that contains most of the mathematical routines necessary to perform the statistical calculations needed by professionals working in the social sciences and related fields.

SRAM (es-ram) acronym for Static Random Access Memory, see **static allocation.**

SS/DD see **single-sided** and **double density.**

SS/SD see **single-sided** and **single density.**

stack a list that permits items to be inserted or removed only from one end. Data in a stack is usually handled as a LIFO process so that the last item added is the first to be removed. See also **queue.**

star network a design in which all peripherals (including microcomputers) are connected to one central computer. While the individual computers of this type network may stand alone with their own peripherals, generally, the members of the network draw on the resources of the central computer. See also **bus network, LAN,** and **ring network.**

statement see **instruction.**

static allocation the division of main memory or other system resources in which each process is preassigned a portion before the program is run and the portion does not change during the execution of the program. See also **dynamic allocation.**

status line an area usually at the top or bottom of the CRT screen that provides information on the current operation of the software in use.

storage see **auxiliary storage.**

store to place in main memory or auxiliary storage. See also **load, retrieve,** and **save.**

streamer tape a moderate-speed tape system most commonly used as backup for a hard disk. These tapes offer a storage capacity equivalent to a small hard disk.

string a set of characters treated as a unit.

structured programming a method of writing instructions that emphasizes orderly development of a program as a series of modules that will accept, process, and output data to and from other modules or a system device as processing proceeds by a specific set of guidelines. See also **heuristic** and **modular program.**

subdirectory a directory that is listed as part of another directory.

subroutine a set of instructions that is repeated several times within a program or needed by several different programs.

supercomputer a very large, extremely fast, and powerful computer that is capable of handling very complex problems and vast amounts of data.

Relatively few supercomputers are built each year, and these are normally custom-designed for a specific application.

surge protector an electrical device designed to eliminate **voltage spikes** from the input power source. See also **power conditioner.**

switched line see **dial-up line.**

synchronous characterized by operations guided by regularly timed signals. See also **asynchronous.**

system clock a clock within the computer that keeps track of the correct time and date. Such a clock is commonly used by the operating system to place the current date and time mark on files in the directory lists and by many programs such as reminders, calendars, and timers. This should not be confused with the **clock speed,** which is a measure of how fast the computer's microprocessor works.

system software programs required for the basic operation of the computer and its components. See also **application software, procedure-oriented,** and **user-oriented.**

system utilities programs usually supplied as part of the system software that permit and assist in basic control and maintenance of the computer and its components.

T

table an ordered arrangement of data, often presented in rows and columns. See also **array.**

tablet an input device used for graphics applications. Tablets consist of a touch-sensitive membrane, pressure on which (using a stylus or even a finger) is transferred to the corresponding position on the screen.

tape a system of data storage using a series of parallel tracks or channels on which files are stored in a predetermined and rigid sequence. Updating or changing tapes requires making a new copy of the entire tape. Tape systems include simple cassettes, relatively fast streamer tapes, VCR systems, digital audiotape systems (DATS), and high-speed reel-to-reel units.

TB abbreviation for **terabyte.**

telecommunications the communications between devices that are not located near each other and must make use of a data communications channel. This occurs when terminals (including other computers) link to a host computer for an exchange of data.

template a device used as a guide. Two common examples of templates that are used with computers are a *keyboard template,* which acts as a label for certain keys to identify their function and a *file template,* which is somewhat similar to a form letter permitting the user to simply fill in the blanks.

tera- a prefix meaning 1 trillion.

terabyte 1 trillion bytes.

terminal any device that acts as an input/output unit for a computer. Terminals most often have a keyboard and a CRT screen or printer but may be in many designs.

thermal printer one that produces images by using heat interaction with the paper.

thimble a type of printwheel similar to a daisy-wheel but with curved spokes so that it looks like a thimble.

32-bit processor a microprocessor that handles data in 32-bit blocks and is faster than the 16-bit models and much older and slower than 8-bit machines. An increasing number of computers are using 32-bit processors.

throughput the amount of work done in a given amount of time by a computer or a component of a system such as a printer. For example, throughput for a printer would be measured by the number of pages printed in a given amount of time.

time-sharing a method of processing used in multiprogramming that shares the CPU time between two or more processes. With rapid processing speeds, the CPU can alternate between the processes without any significant loss in speed. See also **multiprocessing** and **multitasking.**

toggle 1. a switch or control code that turns an action on and off by repeated action or use. 2. to turn something on and off by repeating the same action.

touch-sensitive keyboard a type of button arrangement rarely found on computers but seen on some calculators. It is basically a touch-sensitive membrane that is very sensitive to contact and requires very little pressure to "press" a key. This type of keyboard may be satisfactory when only limited keyboard use is expected. See also **full-stroke key** and **limited-stroke key.**

touch-sensitive membrane consists of a smooth imprinted surface covering a series of sensitive switches or other sensing devices on which a small pressure in the proper place will activate the desired action. Few computers use these for full keyboards, but they are found as tablets and as special function areas on some keyboards.

tpi abbreviation for **tracks per inch,** a measure of data density of disks.

track   1. a circular pattern used for recording data on a disk. 2. a data channel on a magnetic tape.

track ball   a device similar to a mouse, which uses a ball mounted on a fixed base to control cursor movement, action on the screen, and object placement. The ball is rolled with the fingers or palm, and the movement on the screen corresponds to the direction of the ball's motion. Track balls are most commonly used in applications such as games and graphics.

tractor feed   a method of moving paper through a printer that uses a series of pins on either side of an adjustable-width mechanism. This method is recommended whenever a large throughput is anticipated or variable-width paper is used. See also **friction feed, pin feed,** and **sheet feeder.**

transient   temporary; a *transient program,* for example, is one that is not in memory or storage permanently.

translator   a program that changes another program from one form to another, such as converting a program written by humans into a form that the computer can understand (usually a necessary step). See also **assembler, compiler,** and **interpreter.**

transparent   indicates that a program in memory does not affect (is *transparent* to) all other operations, even though it may have an effect on them. With a transparent program present in memory, the user may still interact with the operating system and run other programs in the normal way.

TSR   abbreviation for **terminate and stay resident,** a program that remains in main memory after it has run.

turnkey system   a ready-to-use system, usually supplied by a single vendor, that includes hardware, software, and training.

U

ultra-density   see **high-density.**

uninterruptible power supply   see **UPS.**

UNIX   a popular operating system that employs **shells** and **pipelines.** Although UNIX is found mostly on large systems, a few emulators are available for microcomputers, and a few have UNIX-like operating systems. See also **XENIX.**

UPC   abbreviation for **universal product code,** a familiar bar code found on many products in food, drug, and other stores.

update   the process of changing software or hardware to a newer version. See also **upgrade.**

upgrade   the process of changing software or hardware to a more *powerful* version. See also **update.**

upload   to transfer a copy of a file from a small computer, usually a microcomputer, to a host computer. See also **download.**

UPS   abbreviation for **uninterruptible power supply,** an electrical device that contains a battery pack and will supply enough power to a system in the event of a power failure, permitting it to be shut down in an orderly manner.

user-friendly   easy to understand and use.

user-oriented   describes a program or system that is designed to expedite its use for its intended purpose. For example, a high-level programming language is normally user-oriented. See also **application software, procedure-oriented,** and **system software.**

user-programmable key   see **function key.**

user-readable format   any display that you can read, such as on a screen or printed page. See also **machine-readable format.**

user-supported software   see **shareware.**

V

vaporware   hardware or software products that are announced by a company but do not appear on the market for a very long time, if ever.

variable fonts   the ability of a device such as a printer to offer more than one print typeface or style.

variable pitch   the ability of a device such as a printer to offer more than one print size.

VDT   abbreviation for **video display terminal,** any device used to give a visual display of computer output, such as on a screen. For personal computers this is most commonly a single CRT unit called a monitor.

vendor   a supplier of computer hardware or software.

VGA card   IBM's **Video Graphics Array,** an advanced, high-resolution color graphics system designed for professional applications on its top-line PCs. See also **CGA card, EGA card, Hercules card,** and **MDPA card.**

video display terminal   see **VDT.**

virtual drive   a logical drive that is set up to reside in main memory.

virtual memory   the use of segmentation or disk file overlays to make the total amount of available memory appear to be larger and hold more than its actual capacity would permit.

VLSI   abbreviation for **very large scale integration,** refers to circuits first developed in the mid-1970s that permitted hundreds of thousands of electrical components to be placed on a single board. Such chips could contain an entire microprocessor and were the basis for the modern microcomputer.

voice recognition   the ability of a computer to accept input commands or data using the spoken word.

voice synthesizer   see **speech synthesizer.**

volatile   a main memory or auxiliary storage design in which the stored data is lost when the power is removed from the system. See also **nonvolatile.**

voltage spike   a sudden jump in electrical power. These can be very dangerous to data and, if large enough, to computer hardware as well. See also **power conditioner** and **surge protector.**

volume   see **logical drive.**

VSAM   (vee-sam) acronym for **V**irtual **S**torage **A**ccess **M**ethod, a method of organizing a file that permits random and sequential access of each record. The VSAM technique was developed for IBM mainframes and has the advantage that it is hardware-independent in that the data is not stored or retrieved according to the normal cylinder and track method.

W

wait state   a halt in the execution of a program during which an input/output or other operation is performed.

warm boot   to bring a system into operation from the keyboard; this method does not clear the memory of the system and is used most often to interrupt a process without losing what is in memory. See also **cold boot.**

wildcard   a generic symbol (such as * or ?) that can stand for either a single character or for several characters. Wildcards are frequently used in system commands.

Winchester disk system   a high-speed, high-density hard disk storage system that employs an airtight fixed disk on which the read/write heads lightly glide. Such systems are very reliable and do not experience head crashes.

window   a portion of the screen set aside for a specific display or purpose. See also **split screen.**

word   a group of bits treated as a unit of storage. Most microcomputers use 16-bit words, but some older ones are 8-bit machines and an increasing number of 32-bit systems are becoming available. Larger computers may use 64-bit or larger words.

word processor   a software package consisting of programs designed to accept and process normal text (words) as data. Such programs may range from simple systems that are little more than a limited line editor to those with complex screen handling, editing, enhancements, and assistance features.

word wrap   a feature of most word processors in which the text is automatically continued from one line to the next.

write-protected   cannot be written to or changed. See also **R/O.**

write-protect notch   a notch on the side of a floppy disk that prevents the data from being altered. The 5¼-inch diskettes are write-protected by covering the notch with a write-protect tab. The reverse system is used for 8-inch diskettes.

write-protect tab   a small strip of opaque tape used on the write-protect notch on some diskettes to provide write-protection.

WYSIWYG   (wiz-ee-wig) acronym for **W**hat **Y**ou **S**ee **I**s **W**hat **Y**ou **G**et.

X

XENIX   a version of **UNIX** found on some powerful microcomputers.

XT   an older *IBM PC.*

Index